For Beginners LLC
62 East Starrs Plain Road
Danbury, CT 06810 USA
www.forbeginnersbooks.com

Text: © 2000 Jim Powell
Illustrations: © 2000 Joe Lee
Cover Design: Renée Michaels
Cover Illustration: Joe Lee

A For Beginners® Documentary Comic Book
Originally published by Writers and Readers, Inc.
Copyright © 2000

Cataloging-in-publication information is available from the Library of Congress.

ISBN-10 # 1-934389-07-2 Trade
ISBN-13 # 978-1-934389-07-2 Trade

Manufactured in the United States of America

For Beginners® and Beginners Documentary Comic Books® are published
by For Beginners LLC.

Reprint Edition

TABLE OF CONTENTS

INTRODUCTION

*H*undreds of years before Kipling wrote: "East is East and West is West, and never the twain shall meet," East and West had been encountering each other. There were, of course, barriers. It was hard, for instance, to walk, ride a horse, or sail from Europe to Asia—especially when you had to cross towering mountain ranges, thick belts of jungle, empty wastes of desert, and vast uncharted stretches of ocean. But these obstacles did not discourage such early explorers as Megasthenes and Marco Polo.

These men brought back fantastic tales: of wise men who prayed in the water naked, of gymnosophists (yogis) who subsisted on fragrances rather than foods, and who worshipped cows; of kings who had thousands of wives, one each night for 1,000 nights; of great snails so large that three or four men could shelter in their shells (tortoises); of huge horses with gigantic ears, teeth, and noses that reached to the ground (elephants), of people who washed the walls of their houses with cow dung, who killed nothing and ate no flesh, but subsisted on roots, rice, and milk; of folk who worshipped idols—some shaped like cows, some like monkeys, some like buffaloes, some like peacocks; of regions where the men and women went about virtually naked, with a cloth bound round their middle, and no other apparel; where the girls married at age five or six; where merchants did a great traffic in spices, silk, sandalwood, and sugar; where there grew a species of tree that bore fruit, wine, oil, sugar, vinegar, cords, coals, thatch, sails for ships, mats to sit or lie on, wood for houses, brooms for sweeping, and beams for building ships (the coconut palm).

All this they wrote of India. Of China and Japan, their stories seemed equally bizarre.

Like Alice in Wonderland encountering the hookah-smoking Caterpillar, the West has long regarded the East as an exotic Other. But this Other was dark, feminine, mysterious, and submissive—an Oriental Other with tremulous gazelle-like eyes dark as lotus blossoms; alluring, dark-nippled breasts; an undulant dark-limbed body; nectar-like lips; smooth thighs; deep navel; flowing hair; breath fragrant as flowers of paradise, voice soft as liquified moonlight; and a mouth sweet as mango.

This image created an innacurate picture of the Orient, a misrepresentation that attempted to sum up an entire swath of geography and cultures stretching from the cedars of Lebanon to the Zen temples of Japan. The image sought to shape this huge, unknowable mystery into something knowable and known, dreamily feminine and submissive. By producing such images, the West began to imagine and fantasize a feminine Orient, an amorous Orient, a passive, subjective, introverted, and weak Orient—a dark love-bunny Orient unable to speak for herself, but in need of a Western voice for expression.

And what a voice the West gave the Orient!

When, for example, in the Divine Comedy, Dante wrote of Mohammed, the poet depicted him inhabiting one of the lowest regions of Hell. There Mohammed is punished by being eternally sliced in twain from his anus to the top of this head!

Alice: His sin?

Caterpillar: Being a false prophet.

But if Westerners underrated "the Orient," they overrated it as well. Western scholars typically showed interest in the Classical Eras and Golden Ages of Eastern civilizations—their great scriptures, works of art, philosophies, and religions. They were never so interested in their Oriental contemporaries: their hopes, desires, sufferings, and uniqueness.

And it is much the same today. Orientalists still tend to study the great philosophies of the East. Western orientalists know more about the great historical past of the Orient than most inhabitants of the Orient.

The Western orientalist imagines the Orient as eternal, unchanging, exotic, sexually insatiable, mystical, passive, subjective, introverted, spiritual, weak, primitive, mute, and silent. On the other hand, he imagines the West as virile, masculine, powerful, materialistic, extroverted, analytic, and objective.

Alice: Aren't these just clichés and stereotypes?

Yes, but it was not until the 1980s that most scholars of the Orient realized that they had been creating a set of fantasies about the East. In his book entitled Orientalism, Edward Said pointed out many of the West's unexamined attitudes towards the East. He demonstrated how these fantasies and beliefs formed the basis for Western colonial enterprises in the East. For generations Western scholars of the Orient had generalized about "the Oriental mind" or the "Indian mind" or the "Hindoo mind."

Only recently has the East started writing—and painting and sculpting—back against the West, countering the West's misrepresentations of "the East." No longer does the "mute Orient" need the Western scholar to speak for it.

The Philosophies & Religions Of India

ndia. The very name conjures up images of snowy Himalayan peaks that seem to rise even higher than the moon's orbit, of icy waters tumbling swiftly over dizzying precipices, of deep, thunder-voiced waterfalls blending in with the growling of young bears in their caves, of breezes bellowing through stands of bamboo, of the drone of bees intoxicated with sips of sweet mango blossoms, and of the resonant mantras of yogis chanting in their caves.

Just as the Himalayan summits rise up as the measure of all mountains, for many Western thinkers, Indian spirituality—exemplified by the meditations of yogis in their caves—has come to represent the peak of Indian culture. Yet there is a problem with these kinds of images. For Westerners have thought of India as a land of Gods sitting serenely atop pink lotuses floating on the cosmic waters; of Gods who have magically sprouted 3 heads and 5,000 arms; of naked fakirs sleeping on beds of nails; of snake charmers mesmerizing dark-hooded cobras; of elephants bathing in the moonlight; of turbaned rajas twiddling their dark, ornate mustaches while entwined with their lovers in impossible knots of flesh; of swarms of sagacious sahibs, worshippers, and sadhus swallowing sweetmeats.

The problem is that these are all Hindu images. And although introductions to Indian philosophy tend to center on Hinduism, India is far from being all Hindu. Verily, Hindus make up only about 60 percent of a diverse population of over 400 distinct religious communities. The waters flowing down from those Himalayan peaks quench the thirst not only of Hindus, but of Jews, Parsis, Jains, Sikhs, Buddhists, Christians, and Muslims—to name just a few.

And just as the United States, Australia, and New Zealand harbor native populations celebrating their own religions and philosophies, and speaking their own languages, India teems with a million tribal peoples speaking their own unique tongues and worshipping in distinct ways. India's population speaks 325 languages, representing 12 language families. India, in other words, is so ragtag, so multiform, that one does it violence by attempting to reduce it to a single, Hindu culture.

Geography has been a major force in the shaping of Indian religion and philosophy. For the subcontinent of India hangs like a giant triangle from the underbelly of Asia: To the north and northwest tower some of the world's highest mountains, the Himalayas, the Hindu Kush, and the Sulaiman ranges. Eastward, dense tracts of jungle present an impenetrable barrier. A coastline humming with breakers pulsing in from the vast expanses of the Indian Ocean embraces the remainder of the subcontinent. For thousands of years these natural barriers discouraged foreign invaders from all but one direction: the West. Kipling's famous line "East is East and West is West, and never the twain shall meet," was possible only because a great Western power—the British Empire—did meet India, and conquered her. And similar meetings have been taking place for thousands of years. As each wave of Western invaders entered the subcontinent, Indian religion and philosophy changed.

Indian philosophy, is something like a banyan tree. Called "The Many-footed," banyans, for thousands of years, have provided shade, forming natural outdoor meeting rooms that have acted as schools, temples, and marketplaces.

The banyan begins its life as a single trunk that rises from a tiny seed. Yet its widespreading branches eventually form a vast canopy, spreading out to shade an entire acre. As these branches expand outward, they send down aerial roots that reach the ground, penetrate it, and become secondary trunks, often rivaling the original trunk in size. So substantial are these aerial root-trunks, that often one cannot distinguish them from the original.

The six trunks forming the basis of Indian religious and philosophical thought are, in historical order, as follows:

<u>The Indus Valley Trunk (c. 3000-1500 B.C.)</u>
<u>The Indo-Brahmanical Trunk (c. 1500-600 B.C.)</u>
<u>The Indo-Shramanical Trunk (c. 600 B.C.-300 A.D.)</u>
<u>The Indic (Hindu, Buddhist, Jain) Trunk (c. 300-1200 A.D.)</u>
<u>The Indo-Islamic Trunk (c. 1200-1757 A.D.)</u>
<u>The Indo-Anglican Trunk (c. 1757-present)</u>

The entire lush, tangled canopy of Indian religious and philosophical systems with all its Gods and Goddesses, images, and symbols, rests atop these major trunks. What's more, this banyan tree of Indian religions and philosophies is a **talking tree**. It talks to itself, and has been doing so for thousands of years. For religion and philosophy, in India, have never been a single, unified tree. This talking tree sounds and resounds with the ongoing conversations, snippets of gossip, polemics, arguments, criticisms, and plagiarisms each trunk has exchanged with all the others, down through the ages.

THE INDUS VALLEY TRUNK
(c. 3000-1500 B.C.)

INDUS VALLEY, INC.

The word "Hindu" was originally a Persian term for the area of the Indus River. Then, Alexander the Great called the people who lived on the banks of the Indus Hindus.

However, long before Alexander the Great came to India—long before Hinduism existed—an ancient civilization thrived on the banks of the Indus. Scholars know very little about this ancient Indus Valley civilization. They do know that, like the ancient civilizations of Egypt and Mesopotamia, the settlement flourished because it lay in a great river valley. From about 3000 B.C. to about 1500 B.C, it covered 750,000 square miles. Then, suddenly, it disappeared.

Its two largest cities, Mohenjo-Daro and Harrapa, sheltered some 80,000 inhabitants in orderly, streets laid out in an east-west/north-south grid. The citizens enjoyed the benefits of a public drainage system, municipal wells, and even public garbage collection. Everything was so uniform that even the size of the bricks from which the houses were built were the same.

> BUT NOTHING CAME BEFORE ME. DID IT?

HARAPPA'S BAZAAR

Fortified citadels, sitting atop raised mounds, crowned both Mohenjo-Daro and Harrapa. Surrounding these were government halls and temples. The view from these raised citadels took in streets teeming with shoppers. In fact, the great bazaars of Harappa and Mohenjo-Daro, seemed to have served the same function in the ancient world as shopping malls do today. And it was through their arts and economic power—rather than arms—that their influence spread. Archaeologists have found very few weapons, but lots of intricate jewelry made of shells from the Gulf of Oman, gold from Afghanistan, and copper from far inland. These artifacts indicate that the bazaars sat in the very hub of a vast network of trade routes. Evidently, their artisans were wonderfully skilled.

What little we know of the religion and philosophy of the Indus Valley is based on the temples and various objects within them. These temples surrounded vast central courtyards with large central bathing areas for ritual bathing. Flanking the bathing areas were brick platforms—possibly used for ritual altars. Archaeologists have unearthed large numbers of lithe terra-cotta figurines, possibly goddesses, and numerous soapstone seals inscribed with a script that no one has yet convincingly deciphered.

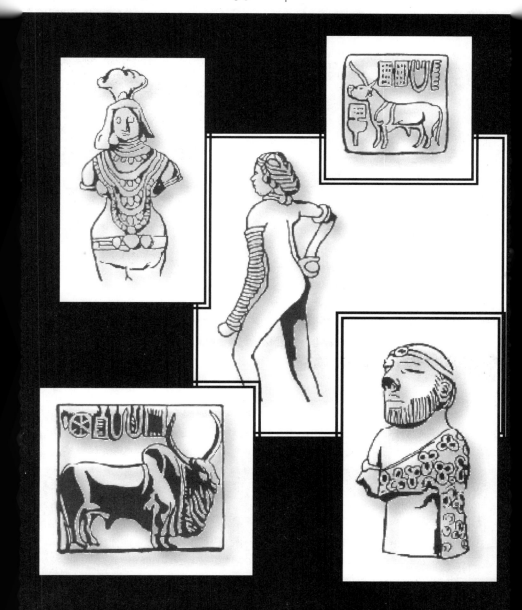

On one of these seals, however, is the image of a horned figure positioned in what appears to be a yogic posture. The figure, which has three faces, looks out on a veritable zoo of animals, which surround him. Is he, as some scholars argue, an early form of the Hindu God *Shiva*, Supreme Yogi, Lord of Creatures? Nobody knows.

Archaeologists have also unearthed large numbers of polished stone phalli. Many of these elements:

※ **ritual bathing**

※ **altars**

※ **goddess worship**

※ **a yoga god surrounded by animals**

※ **phallus worship**

※ **a concern for social order**

※ **architecture laid out in an east-west grid**

are found in what later would be called Hinduism.

Alice: What happened in between?
Caterpillar: Well, that brings us to our next trunk—the Indo-Brahmanical.

The Indo-Brahmanical Trunk
(c. 1500–600 B.C.)

Alice: Indo-Brahmanical?
Caterpillar: The **Brahmans** were the priests of the Aryan tribes.
Alice: Aryan tribes?

THE ARYANS

Aryan means "Noble One." Whenever a group of people think of themselves in this way, it is generally not very good news for other "non-noble" people.

The Aryans were fair-skinned Caucasians. For decades scholars have tried to figure out where these wandering herdsmen and warriors came from, and when, but they left behind no historical records. It seems they had a homeland, possibly in the oak-forested Russian steppes. But they left their homelands, some traveling north and west, establishing Athens in Greece. Others ventured as far as what is now Spain, and another group migrated into what is now England and Ireland. Still another pushed into Persia, where they established an empire.

No one knows for sure the exact history of the Aryans in India. The best guess is that around 1500 B.C. waves of these hostile nomads spilled into the Indian subcontinent from the northwest, through the passes of the Hindu Kush mountains of Afghanistan and into the valley of the Indus River. Scholars used to think the Aryans destroyed the Indus Valley civilization, but now believe that the Indus Valley civilization disappeared all on its own.

These invaders spoke a dialect of **Indo-European**. It would eventually evolve into **Sanskrit**, the ancient language of India.

Alice: Indo-European? Sanskrit?

Caterpillar: The Indo-European family tree of languages has as its trunk a language called **Proto-Indo European**. This is an ancient tongue spoken by that loose group of tribes inhabiting the ancient oak-forested Russian steppes. Around 2500 B.C. they dispersed—one branch spreading in conquering waves across Europe-and the other driving southward through Iran and Afghanistan into India.

Alice: Does this mean that Greek, Latin, Old High German, and Sanskrit are just daughters of the Proto-Indo-European mother tongue?

Caterpillar: That is what linguists have proven. For instance, they found similarities between Sanskrit and such distantly related Indo-European tongues as Lithuanian, Latin, Irish, Persian, and English.

Alice: Really?

Caterpillar: Yes. For instance, the Lithuanian proverb "God gave teeth; God will give bread," reads almost the same in Lithuanian, Sanskrit, and Latin:

LATIN: Deus dedit dentis; Deus dabit panem

LITHUANIAN: Dievas dave dantis; Dievas duos duonos

SANSKRIT: Devas adadat datas; Devas dat dhanas

Alice: That's remarkable!

Caterpillar: Another example: The Sanskrit word, **Aryan**, the Irish word **Erin** (the ancient name of Ireland), and the Persian word **Iran**, all branch out from an ancient Proto-Indo-European word. The Sanskrit word for ship is **naus**, which corresponds to the English words **nau**tical and **nav**igation.

A god is a **deva**—which relates to our word **div**inity. Knowledge in Sanskrit is called **Jnana**, which relates to our word **gno**sis, **Gno**stic and **kno**wledge. The number **three** in Sanskrit is **tri.** Our word for **father**, which is **pater** in both Latin and Greek, is **pitar** in Sanskrit. Our word for **sweat** is **svet** in Sanskrit.

And just as there are linguistic similarities be-

tween Indo-European languages, there are also likenesses among Indo-European myths.

For instance: The Greek God **Zeus**, the big guy in the sky with the big muscles and the thunderbolt, is the equivalent of the Roman God **Jupiter** and the Indian God **Dyus Pitar**. All of them hang out in the sky, look like Rambo, and wield a thunderbolt.

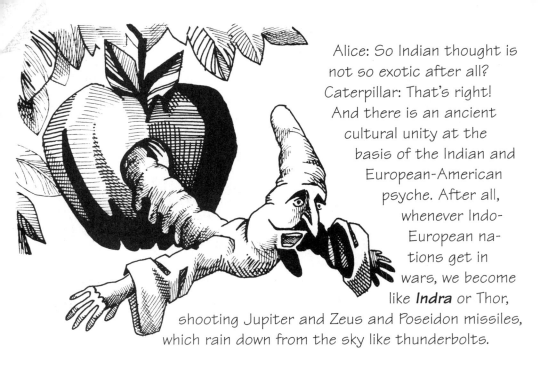

Alice: So Indian thought is not so exotic after all?
Caterpillar: That's right! And there is an ancient cultural unity at the basis of the Indian and European-American psyche. After all, whenever Indo-European nations get in wars, we become like **Indra** or Thor, shooting Jupiter and Zeus and Poseidon missiles, which rain down from the sky like thunderbolts.

Yet Sanskrit, the language of the Indo-Aryans, is also quite different from English. It paints a view that life is based on **essences**. For instance, in English we say:

The **apple** is getting **ripe**.

For us, the apple itself is the important thing, and its being ripe, is merely a characteristic a secondary quality.

But in Sanskrit, we would say:

The **apple** goes to **ripeness**.

In Sanskrit, ripeness is a universal essence to which apples, pears, mangoes—any fruit—must evolve.

And just as ripeness is a universal essence to which fruit matures, for the Hindu, there is a universal essence within the whole universe. But this is an abstract, **spiritual** essence.

Yet, individual things are important only if they mirror this abstract essence of the universe. Thus, for the Hindu, the lives of individual human beings, or the precise design for the layout of a temple or a city, the swelling sounds of a musical composition, the sensuous volumes of a sculpture, or the "flavor" of a poem all possess an essence.

Alice: Then what is the essence of a Hindu temple?

Caterpillar: Hindu temples, houses, and towns are all based on a geometric pattern called the **vastu-purusha mandala**:

The **inner square**, the essence, represents **Brahma, The Creator** of the universe. And it lies at the absolute spiritual **core** of the temple. The temple, in turn, sits at the precise **center** of the town, which rests in the exact **midpoint** of the country. Thus, the spiritual essence of the temple is the essence of the town, and the whole country!

Even Indian poetry has an essence—or **rasa**:

**She, with eyes dark as water lilies
has full breasts, golden in hue,
with black nipples, pressed
so closely together, not even
the fiber of a lotus
can find space between.**

Īśāna				Sūrya				Agni
25	26	27	28	29	30	31	32	1
24								2
23			Pṛthvidhāra					3
22								4
Kubera 21	Mitra			Brahmā		Śaśi		5 Yama
20								6
19								7
18			Vivasvān					8
17	16	15	14	13	12	11	10	9
Vāyu				Varuṇa				Nirṛti

Just as an Indian herbalist might mix essential oils of sandalwood and musk, an Indian poet might at times blend poetic essences. The essence ("flavor," "sap" or rasa) of this poem is a blend of the **devotional** and the **erotic** sentiments. Even though it describes a goddess, **Uma, The Golden One**, in devotional terms, the poem is suffused, like a dark lotus, with erotic sap.

Alice: That's poetic!

Caterpillar: Well, the Vedic .s were a poetic bunch. So most of Hinduism is poetic because most of Hinduism springs from the **Vedas**.

Alice: The Vedas?

Caterpillar: The Vedas, according to most orthodox Hindus, are eternal, nonhuman in origin, and contain all knowledge. When you hear them, they sound like a bunch of chants. Ancient wise men called **rishis**—or **seers**—heard and saw the Vedas in their visions.

While Hindus accept the Vedas as a timeless revelation, Western scholars of India have learned that they took centuries to be composed. During this long period, society, religion, and even the Sanskrit language of the Vedas changed considerably, in the same way that Shakespeare sounds different than English rap.

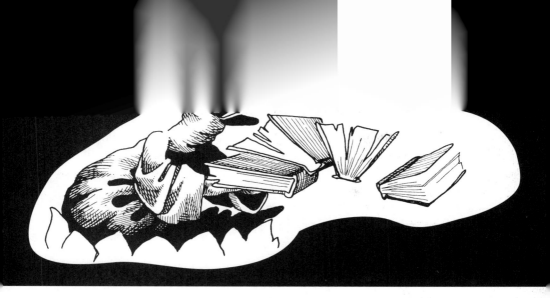

Alice: Well, then, how can the Vedas be eternal?

Caterpillar: The two notions do not rule each other out. It is remotely possible that the Vedas could be eternal, but revealed to the visions of seers in different times.

Alice: How many Vedas are there?

There are four Vedas: **Rig Veda, Sama Veda, Yajur Veda,** and **Atharva Veda.** The Rig Veda (**Hymn Veda**) is a collection of ten books (**mandalas**) of sacred utterances (**mantras**) used to invoke various deities (**devas**). The Sama Veda (**Chant Veda**) is a collection of chants (**saman**) based on the Rig Veda. The Yajur Veda (**Instruction Veda**) contains instructions for performing Vedic rituals. The Atharva Veda (**Magical Spell Veda**) is a collection of incantations, chants and spells. These are used for curing disease, for finding a spouse, for killing an enemy, etc.

Alice: But then what are the Vedas?

Caterpillar: Veda means knowledge.

Alice: Knowledge of what?

Caterpillar: Knowledge of how to invoke the Vedic Gods. The purpose of Vedic ritual was to support, enliven, and nourish the Gods or devas. In turn, the devas would bestow wealth (in the form of cattle), happiness, and long life to the sacrificers. Moreover, in the Vedic worldview, this mutual admiration society between Gods and men is what sustains Cosmic Order (**rita**).

The Vedic sacrifices also served a social function. Because they required the sacrifice of horses, cattle, goats, sheep, ghee, milk, and grains, they were costly affairs. The ability to afford a sacrifice marked the sacrificer as a person of wealth. Thus, performing sacrifices was a status symbol in Vedic society. Only the higher classes were able to afford these rituals.

Alice: Who were the Vedic Gods?

Well, especially important was Agni, which literally means "fire." After all, during Vedic sacrifices, various materials such as ghee, animals, and grains were offered into a fire, which carried these burnt offerings to heaven. Another important god was Indra, an atmospheric warrior who assisted the Vedic peoples in their battles. There were also many fertility gods.

ENOUGH WITH THIS SACRIFICE, COULD I BECOME SACRED ALREADY?

SAY WHAT?!

Alice: Well then, we have a priestly god (Agni), a warrior god (Indra), and many fertility gods—does this say anything about the make-up of Vedic society?

Caterpillar: Yes, since religion philosophy and myth are always a reflection of society. Vedic society was made up of three main classes: priests (Brahmans), warriors, and people who farmed and herded.

Alice: What was Vedic ritual like?

Caterpillar: One of the most important rituals was the Horse Sacrifice, or **Ashvamedha**. This ritual could only be commissioned by a king. The Brahman priests would select a mighty, virile stallion, and let it roam about for an entire year. There was only one catch. This horse would have to remain a celibate horse. He could not emit semen for the entire year. No horsing around with any mares it might encounter. Everywhere the horse roamed would become the land of the king. If the horse wandered into another kingdom, then the disputed land would often be settled by war.

After one year, the horse was brought back to the Brahman priests. They would prepare the sacrificial altar, then strangle the horse to death. Next, the king's wife would have ritual sex with the dead stallion.

Alice: Oh baby!

Caterpillar: The divine power of the horse (in the form of his stored-up semen) would then symbolically enter the queen, and thereby strengthen the king and all the people in the kingdom.

Alice: What does this have to do with Hinduism being about essences?

Caterpillar: Well, a stallion's semen is his essence.

Alice: Is the stallion's semen, then, the essence of the ritual?

Caterpillar: No, the essence of the ritual, and of all the Vedas, is the **Sacred Utterance, Speech, mantra,** the **Word**. In fact, in the Vedic universe, Speech is a goddess, **Vac**. The living body of this Goddess is the sacred chant, the mantra. When She is properly treated, She makes the ritual work unfailingly. The **Word, Vac,** when properly pronounced, influences the Vedic Gods to fulfill your desires: making a particular person love you, curing your fever, or killing your enemy.

Alice: Well, if the Word is the essence of the Veda, then what is the essence of the Word?

Caterpillar: The Vedas proclaim that their own chants and syllables are but manifestations of a **transcendental, supreme ether**.

Alice: Supreme ether?

Yes. The Vedas and all the Gods and Goddesses spring from a spiritual essence, a supreme ether. Thus, if you can know that essence, then you can have mastery over the whole Vedic universe. Though the Vedas do mention that they spring from a supreme **transcendental** *essence, this idea is not well-developed in the Vedas. Certainly, over time the Vedic rituals became more and more elaborate, complicated, and expensive. During this time, the Vedic people conquered most of Northern India. However—they forgot the meaning of the Vedas!*

So, towards the end of the **Indo-Brahmanical** period, the priests began writing lengthy prose commentaries on each Veda, explaining and analyzing it. But the Brahmanas not only commented on the Vedic rituals, they contained early speculations about their **meaning** and **purpose**. This philosophical tendency gained momentum, leading to the composition of the **Aranyakas** (Forest Teachings) and the **Upanishads**.

Alice: So the Brahmanas, Aranyakas, and Upanishads begin to **philosophize** about the role of Vedic ritual?

Caterpillar: Yes. Remember, Hinduism is based on the idea of essences. We have seen that the essence of the Veda and its rituals is the Sacred Utterance, the Word, or mantra: Another Sanskrit word for sacred utterance, or prayer, is **bráhman** (with the accent on the first syllable).

A closely related term is **brahmán** (with the accent on the second syllable), which means 'a member of the priestly class.'

> Alice: So a bráhman is a **prayer**, and a brahmán is a **pray-er**, the fellow doing the praying!

Caterpillar: Yes, and the Brahmanas, Aranyakas, and Upanishads began to speculate on the essence of both the prayer (bráhman) and the pray-er (brahmán).

The prayer (**bráhman**) belongs to the outer world, to the world of the Vedic ritual. But this outer ritual is possible only because of **Agni**, **Fire**. And the fire is only possible because of the air or wind. And the air depends upon the sun and moon and the whole Vedic universe. But what is the essence of the universe?

Brahman, the Spirit of the Universe, is the essence of the Vedic universe. This is the essence of the prayer (bráhman).

Alice: But what about the pray-er (brahmán)? Where does that leave him?

Caterpillar: Well they began to speculate about him, also.

In the same way that the prayer is associated with the fire of the ritual, the pray-er has an internal spiritual fire burning inside. This fire is called tapas, a purifying warmth kindled by deep meditation. And just as the external fire of the Vedic ritual depends upon the air or wind, so too does the internal flame depend upon the energy of the yogi's breath. This energy within the meditator's breath is called prana. Just as the external fire of the altar is just a spark of the sun, the inner world of the pray-er is illumined by the sun of knowledge. And just as the external cosmos and the prayer have Brahman as their essence—the personality of the pray-er has an essence, also. It is called the Atman, or the soul.

Alice: Well then, what is the relationship between the Atman and Brahman?

Caterpillar: The Atman IS Brahman. The essence of the external world of the prayer (bráhman) and of the internal word of the pray-er (brahmán) is the **same spiritual essence**!

Thus, the yoga seers of the Upanishads declare:

Aham Brahmasmi!
I am Brahman!
I am the essence of the
entire universe!

This then answers the central question of the Hindu tradition:

"WHO ARE YOU?"

Alice: But if the essence of the pray-er, and of each individual, is the essence of the whole universe, then why does he need all those priests and their rituals?

Caterpillar: That is an excellent question. Truly, it's a question that many of the non-priests began asking—and this sentiment laid the foundation for the next period in the history of Indian religion and philosophy, the **Indo-Shramanical**.

Alice: So, did they stop performing rituals?

Caterpillar: No, as we shall see, Vedic ritual became much less important, but it still survives to this day. For instance, in 1957 a group of India's priests performed a major Vedic sacrifice in order to stop the spread of the hydrogen bomb. Then, in 1970 a group of Indian politicians opposed to the president of India, Indira Gandhi, hired a priest to perform a sacrifice that would kill her.

Alice: Kill her! Well, what happened?

Caterpillar: The priest hired to perform the ritual was, himself, electrocuted to death during the sacrifice he was performing.

Alice: His **karma**, I guess, huh?

Caterpillar: From the standpoint of modern Hinduism, perhaps. But during the era of the **Indo-Brahmanical Period**, Indians had not yet invented the concept of karma. In fact, they were not really Hindu yet. They had managed to provide themselves with some sacred scriptures, the Vedas, along with an elaborate system of rituals to invoke the Vedic Gods.

The Indo-Aryans had established a social order based on the Brahmans or priests at the top, followed by warriors and agriculturists. Finally, as we have discussed, some skeptical, philosophical impulses surfaced during the later part of this era.

However, in that early period, India had not yet built any temples. The Vedic priests practiced all their rituals outside, in the open air. Nobody worshipped a personal God in their heart. There were no pilgrimages, and nobody believed in **karma** or reincarnation. These would have to await another period in Indian history.

Caterpillar: We have seen that a profound crisis began to divide the religious and philosophical life of India during the later period of the Indo-Brahmanical Era. Out of the ashes of the old period, a new period developed, an era based on open skepticism and even antagonism towards the rituals of the Vedic priests. It was from this same skepticism that the Buddhist and Jainist religions philosophies grew.

Some of these antagonisms had already appeared within Brahmanism itself— in texts known as the **Upanishads**.

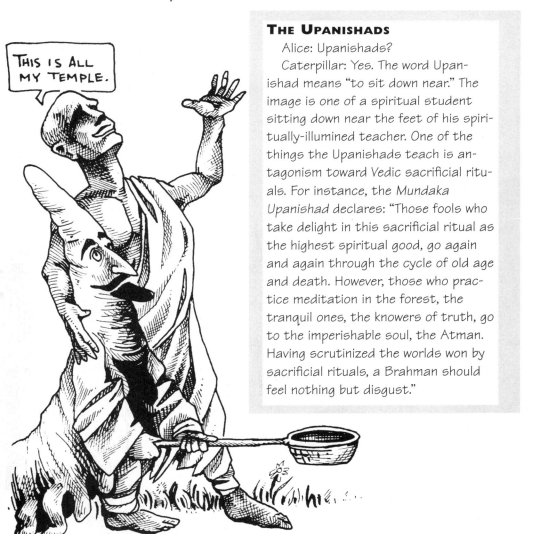

THIS IS ALL MY TEMPLE.

THE UPANISHADS

Alice: Upanishads?

Caterpillar: Yes. The word Upan-ishad means "to sit down near." The image is one of a spiritual student sitting down near the feet of his spiri-tually-illumined teacher. One of the things the Upanishads teach is an-tagonism toward Vedic sacrificial ritu-als. For instance, the *Mundaka Upanishad* declares: "Those fools who take delight in this sacrificial ritual as the highest spiritual good, go again and again through the cycle of old age and death. However, those who prac-tice meditation in the forest, the tranquil ones, the knowers of truth, go to the imperishable soul, the Atman. Having scrutinized the worlds won by sacrificial rituals, a Brahman should feel nothing but disgust."

The authors of the Upanishads challenged the authority of the Brahman, or priestly class. But the main theme of the Upanishads is: what is the essence of the universe? As we have already seen, the Upanishads declare one answer: the essence of the Universe is Brahman. But this Brahman cannot be known through Vedic sacrifice. Rather, Brahman, the essence of the entire universe, is your own **Atman**, your **Self**, the essence of everything.

Alice: What is the **Atman**? How are we to know our own **Self**—our **Atman**?

Caterpillar: According to the Upanishads, we cannot perceive the Atman by touching, by hearing, by seeing, by tasting, by smelling. We cannot even perceive the Atman through the mind. We can only discover the Self in deep meditation. In deep meditation, the meditator discovers that the Atman has three attributes:

- **SAT**: Infinite Being
- **CHIT**: Infinite Consciousness
- **ANANDA**: Infinite Bliss.

As early as the Upanishads, seekers known as **Shramanas** began to seek the inner **Atman through meditation** rather than **through the performance of the ritual sacrifices** of the Brahmans. In fact, traditionally Indians consider Shramanas and Brahmans to be as antagonistic as cats and mice or mongooses and snakes. This is why many scholars consider the philosophical leap from the Vedic sacrifices to the Upanishads as one of the most significant philosophical events in documented history.

The word Shramana means "striver."

Alice: What were they striving to attain?

Caterpillar: Well, about the 6th century B.C., the Indians dreamed up the notions of **reincarnation** and *karma*. Now, karma just means action. If you have bad actions, bad karma, you keep dying and then being reborn, reincarnated into this world until you have good karma. If you have good karma, if you meditate and realize your Atman, then you attain union with Brahman, and escape from the endless round of dying and rebirth.

Alice: But why should anyone not want to be reborn?

Caterpillar: We must remember, the Atman is bliss. It is billions of times more blissful than any earthly pleasures, which, compared to it, are mere suffering. In order to know the Atman, the Shramanas felt that knowledge (*jnana*) is more important than action (*karma*). They cultivated detachment from the material world through ascetic practices. These ascetic practices included celibacy, poverty, fasting, exposing the body to the elements, and other hardships. They also practiced various methods of **yoga**.

Alice: You mean like standing on your head?

Caterpillar: Well, that is just one of the tricks yogis can perform. According to the yogic literature, they are also able to shrink to impossibly small sizes, and then puff up to gigantic proportions.

Alice: What's so funny about that? Even I can do that...watch!

Caterpillar: The biggest trick of all that yoga teaches is the realization of one's own infinite Atman.

The word **yoga** springs from the same root as the English word "yoke." In Sanskrit **yoga** means "union," and the goal of yoga is union with the Atman. Yoga is not an intellectual exercise, because thought cannot fathom the depths of the Atman.

In fact, there is a saying in India: "Yoga should be known by yoga."

GEES, I'D RATHER STAND ON MY HEAD.

Indians practice several types of yoga:

In **mantra-yoga**, the meditator mentally repeats a sound, or mantra. The sound becomes increasingly more refined, like a balloon disappearing into the sky, until it disappears into the Atman.

In **hatha yoga**, the aspirant practices a variety of pretzel-like positions, in order to prepare the body for spiritual practice.

PATANJALI'S EIGHT-LIMBED YOGA

Caterpillar: The classical form of yoga, however, is **Patanjali's raja**, or **royal yoga**. It is also known as **ashtanga**, or **eight-limbed yoga**.

In his *Yoga Sutras*, a collection of aphorisms about yoga philosophy and practice from the 3rd century A.D., **Patanjali** defines yoga as **citta-vritti-nirodha**. That means yoga is "**the cessation of mental fluctuations**."

In other words, the cessation of thoughts. He then proclaims the eight limbs involved in this process:

RESTRAINT (*yama*): this limb includes virtues such as nonviolence (ahimsa), speaking the truth, not stealing, celibacy, and lack of greed.

DISCIPLINE (*niyama*): this limb is embodied by cleanliness, serenity, austerity, self-study, and devotion to God.

POSTURE (*asana*): all that Patanjali says about the posture of the meditator is that it should be firm and comfortable. Obviously, then, Patanjali was not teaching the contorted postures of hatha yoga.

BREATH CONTROL (*pranayama*): the mind can be controlled by controlling the breath.

WITHDRAWAL OF THE FIVE SENSES (*pratyahara*): the yogini, as she enters deeper into her awareness, witnesses that the senses lose awareness of the objects of sight, smell, hearing, touch, and taste. Her mind becomes like a tortoise withdrawing its four limbs and head into its shell.

CONCENTRATION (*dharana*): as the yogini enters even more deeply into her awareness, her mind becomes increasingly focused and concentrated.

MEDITATION (*dhyana*): in this state of meditation, the awareness of the yogini gains stability in an uninterrupted flow of awareness.

ABSORPTION/UNION (*samadhi*): samadhi has two levels. The first level is **samadhi with cognition (*samprajnata samadhi*)**. In this state, there is no division or distinction between the awareness and the object of awareness. Imagine when you are deeply engrossed in a sunset, a painting, a piece of music, or a touch. You are not aware of anything else. Your awareness of your surroundings has vanished. Your awareness of your ego has vanished, and you remain completely absorbed in the object, without distraction. Your mind reflects like a lake at night, only reflecting one thing: the sky. The lake no longer mirrors the trees surrounding the lake, the houses along the shore, the sailboats tied up on the piers, the deer and bear lapping the sweet waters. Only the dark sky appears on the lake's surface.

The second level of samadhi is **samadhi** without cognition (**asamprajnata samadhi**).

Alice: Without cognition?

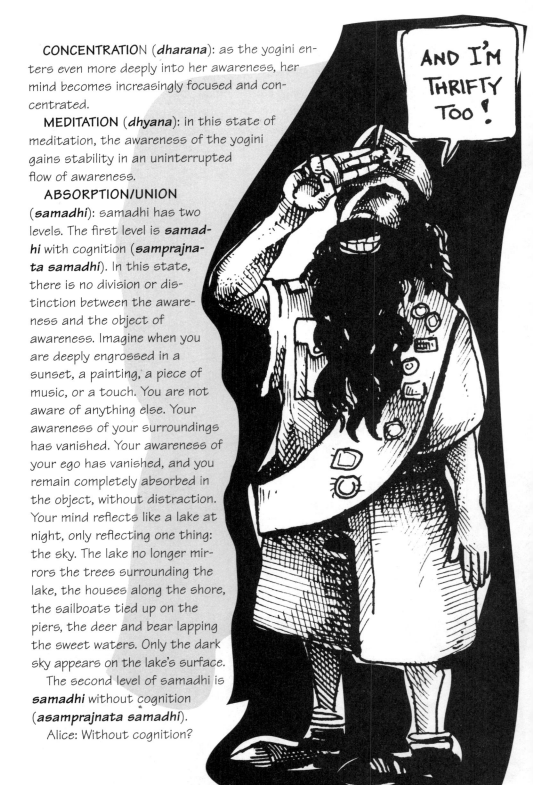

AND I'M THRIFTY TOO!

30

Caterpillar: This just means that in this level of samadhi the object of awareness has simply disappeared. No trace of it remains. Nor is there any awareness of the subject. What remains is pure awareness, **pure consciousness** free of any other object. This is the Atman. When the yogini realizes the Atman, her true nature, she is no longer reborn. It is as if the lake now mirrors nothing at all, but itself.

Alice: Or Brahman!

Caterpillar: Yes, according to the Upanishads, the Atman is like a lake or mirror that reflects Brahman and nothing else.

The goal is a still mind, the cessation of all thoughts. And since the body and breath and mind are so intimately interrelated, the yogini must work on all three. The body becomes still in a firm, comfortable posture, or **asana**. The breath becomes still through **pranayama**, breath control. The mind becomes still through meditation.

When the yogini attains **samadhi,** or union with the **Atman—pure consciousness**—she is no longer aware of body or surroundings, but becomes absorbed in her own **Self**—freed from greed.

Alice: But isn't freedom from greed one of the first steps of Patanjali's yoga?

Caterpillar: Yes. That's why Patanjali does not call them eight **steps** to yoga, but the eight **limbs** of yoga. Because, as anyone knows, the limbs of a child all develop simultaneously. Therefore, celibacy, serenity, truthfulness, and nonviolence do not become perfect until samadhi or union with the Atman becomes perfect.

In samadhi, one is perfectly virtuous. In samadhi, the breath is perfectly controlled—in fact, it ceases. In samadhi, the posture is comfortable, for one's awareness is seated in infinity. In samadhi, concentration and meditation are perfect. So samadhi is the perfection of all the other limbs of yoga.

Alice: Do you have to be a Hindu to practice yoga? I mean, it's, like, taught at the YMCA, isn't it?

That's correct. Nobody knows where yoga came from. For centuries, many Westerners denounced it as overly introverted "navel gazing." Nevertheless, its practice certainly was not confined to Hinduism, or even to India. Still, that is where it first developed, deeply influencing two major Shramana philosophies: Buddhism and Jainism.

JAINISM

Alice: I've never even, like, heard of Jainism!

Caterpillar: Well, it's no wonder! It never gained the vast numbers of followers that Buddhism and Hinduism attracted, yet it exercised a profound influence on the entire world. You see, during the Indo-Shramanical period, folks were freaked out, philosophically speaking. This was partly the result of social conditions. For one thing, the Vedic worldview was tribal, but during the Indo-Shramanical era, towns and cities sprang up all over northern India. And, as everyone knows, cities, by virtue of their size, support individualism.

It's not easy for the member of a tribe to dangle a cigarette from his mouth and hang out at a disco. But if the same dude moves to the city, nobody is going to give him a hard time about his decadent lifestyle. It is not surprising, then, that this era gave birth to a host of free-thinking individuals who rejected the authority of the Vedas and the authority of the Brahman priests.

People also began rejecting the elitist language of the Vedas: Sanskrit. They began to favor instead Prakrit. These Shramana thinkers formed their own independent communities of ascetics.

One such Shramana teacher, named **Purana Kssapa**, believed that virtuous behavior had absolutely no effect on a person's fate. Even if a gal were to wield a razor-sharp weapon and kill everything on earth, she would not be touched by sin. A second freethinker, **Ajita Kesakambala**, was a complete materialist. He did not believe in life after death. A third was an atomist. Atoms, he said, are eternal. Even if a man cuts off another's head with a sharp sword, he actually does no killing, since the sword merely passes between the eternal atoms that make up everything.

NOPE, AIN'T DEAD YET.

Even though these Shramana philosophers were materialists or atomists, they nevertheless practiced some sort of yoga or meditation.

One such Shramana philosopher was the great teacher whom the Jains call **Vardhamana Mahavira, The Great Hero**. According to legend, Mahavira left home at the age of 30 in order to seek salvation. For 12 years he wandered about in the valley of the Ganges River, until, at 42, he achieved perfect enlightenment. At this point, he took off his clothes! He then became known as a conqueror, or *jina*, the word from which the **Jains, The Conquerors**, take their name.

Following their founder's example, Jainism quickly grew into a great society of naked monks, lead by a man called **Bhadrabahu**. Bhadrabahu saw in a vision that a famine was coming, and set out for another province with a great band of naked ascetics. After the famine, he returned, finding that the Jains he had left behind had fallen into all kinds of sinful ways—some of them had even taken to wearing white robes!

Bhadrabahu was so upset with these heretics that he split for Nepal, where he died fasting. He was, however, the only Jain who knew their unwritten scriptures by heart. So, another Jain leader, **Sthulabhadra**, held a meeting with a bunch of monks. They collectively attempted to remember the Jain scriptures, which they called the Eleven Limbs (Anga).

This whole episode caused a great division in Jainism:

On the one hand the **Digambaras** or "space-clad" monks insisted on total nudity, and did not accept the Eleven Limbs as wholly authentic. On the other hand, the **Shvetambaras**, or "white-clad," wore white robes, and accepted the Limbs.

**jiva = SPIRIT
a-jiva = MATTER
jiva/a-jiva . . .
SOUNDS VAGUELY
FAMILIAR .**

Alice: Well, what does Jain philosophy actually teach?

Caterpillar: Jainism is probably much older than Buddhism, and it is probably the group that introduced vegetarianism to India.

Alice: Why?

Caterpillar: They believed that the universe, for each individual, is composed of two things:

**Self (jiva) = Spirit
Not-Self (a-jiva) = Matter

Matter (a-jiva) imprisons Self (jiva) within Matter.**

Alice: How daring! But tell me, what brings about this bondage between jiva and a-jiva?

Caterpillar: It is **karma**, or worldly action that entraps the Self in the Not-Self! In fact, it is **violent actions** especially, such as **killing**, for example, that bind the Self further and further in Matter.

Alice: How naughty!
Well, how does a poor Self, enmeshed in Matter, unbind itself?

Since violence further and further encrusts the soul in matter, salvation or freedom is gained through nonviolence (ahimsa).

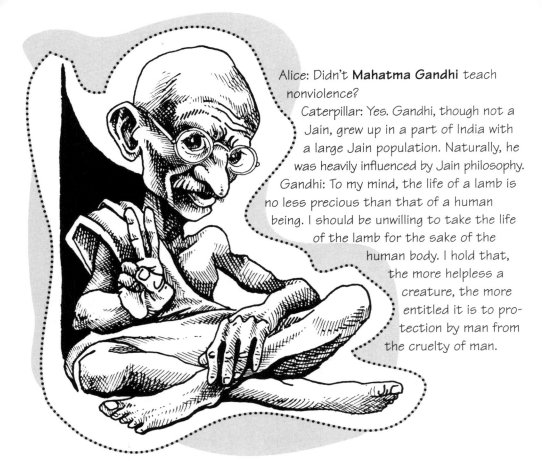

Alice: Didn't **Mahatma Gandhi** teach nonviolence?

Caterpillar: Yes. Gandhi, though not a Jain, grew up in a part of India with a large Jain population. Naturally, he was heavily influenced by Jain philosophy.

Gandhi: To my mind, the life of a lamb is no less precious than that of a human being. I should be unwilling to take the life of the lamb for the sake of the human body. I hold that, the more helpless a creature, the more entitled it is to protection by man from the cruelty of man.

Alice: Are humans the only things that possess Souls?

According to Jains, the whole universe is alive. Plants and animals, turnips, monkeys, ants, fires, rivers, winds—all possess Souls. Every drop of rain, every trembling leaf, every sparkle of light playing across the waters, is alive. Selfish, cruel acts further confine the Soul in Matter. Selfless, generous acts free the Soul from Matter. So, it becomes essential for Jains not to harm other beings, other Souls. Jain monks try to never harm even water, fire, earth, or wind. A Jain monk will let others provide him with food, so that he will not have to kill even a carrot himself. He strains his drinking water, so that he will not kill the bacteria in it. He wears a cloth over his face so that he will not harm the wind when he breathes. He treads ever so lightly on the earth, walking gently, and never running, so as to not harm the Souls in the earth.

Jains believe in a cosmic cycle of time. During the ascending part of the cycle, people grow happier and happier. However, during descending part of the cycle, people grow increasingly more wretched.

Very Happy
Happy
Happy Wretched
Wretched Happy
Wretched
Very Wretched

Alice: What part of the cycle are we in now?

Currently, we are in the Wretched part of the descending phase! So things can only get worse, from a Jain perspective. During the Very Wretched phase, the human life span will only be 20 years. People will only be three feet tall. Humans will have lost all civilization and live in caves. They will even forget how to use fire. This race of runts will commit theft, adultery, murder, and incest, but nobody will think these are sinful. At the very end of the cycle, a fierce storm will kill almost all these runts. Some, however, will survive, and then things will start getting better, and better, and still better. Finally, at the peak of the Very Happy period, things will start going downhill again.

Jains observe special days of fasting-especially on the new and full moons. Once each year, in July, they pay all their debts, confess all their sins, and ask forgiveness of their neighbors for any offense they may have committed.

If a Jain does all of this, her Soul gets free of Matter and she is liberated.

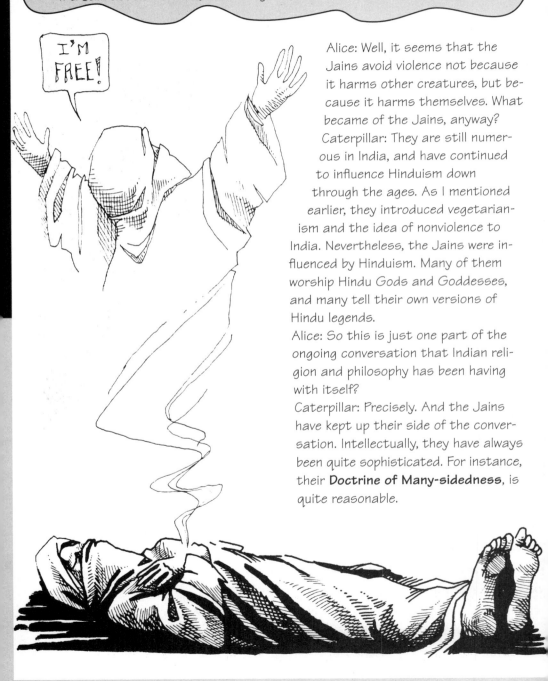

I'M FREE!

Alice: Well, it seems that the Jains avoid violence not because it harms other creatures, but because it harms themselves. What became of the Jains, anyway?

Caterpillar: They are still numerous in India, and have continued to influence Hinduism down through the ages. As I mentioned earlier, they introduced vegetarianism and the idea of nonviolence to India. Nevertheless, the Jains were influenced by Hinduism. Many of them worship Hindu Gods and Goddesses, and many tell their own versions of Hindu legends.

Alice: So this is just one part of the ongoing conversation that Indian religion and philosophy has been having with itself?

Caterpillar: Precisely. And the Jains have kept up their side of the conversation. Intellectually, they have always been quite sophisticated. For instance, their **Doctrine of Many-sidedness**, is quite reasonable.

The Doctrine of Many-sidedness

Alice: Doctrine of Many-sidedness?

The Mad Hatter: Wait a minute! It's my turn! The Doctrine of Many-sidedness (**anekantavada**) is made up of two smaller doctrines:

- **The Doctrine of Maybe**
- **The Doctrine of Viewpoints.**

Alice: I'm feeling a little confused...

The Mad Hatter: I haven't even started yet!

The Doctrine of Maybe

The Mad Hatter: Western logic, beginning with the Greeks, is based on the **law** of the **Excluded Middle.** Either "A" is true, or "A" is not true! Either this **is** an elephant, or it **is not** an elephant!

Western philosophy will admit only **two** possibilities. This gives rise to a **di-lemma.** But **The Doctrine of Maybe** admits **seven** possibilities. This gives rise to a **septa-lemma:**

Alice: A septa-lemma!?

The Mad Hatter: Yes! Seven! And here they are:

ONE: Maybe this **is** an elephant.

TWO: Maybe this **is not** an elephant.

THREE: Maybe this **both is** an elephant, **and not** an elephant!

FOUR: Maybe what it is **indescribable.**

FIVE: Maybe it **is** an elephant, but it is **indescribable.**

SIX: Maybe it **is not** an elephant, and is **indescribable.**

SEVEN: Maybe it **is** an elephant, and **is not** an elephant, and is **indescribable.**

Alice: Oh! I see! So you cannot say absolutely whether something exists or doesn't exist. It only exists or does not from a certain point of view—and points of view are too numerous to be included in any single statement. But what about the **Doctrine of Viewpoints**?

Just who am I really?

The Doctrine of Viewpoints
Caterpillar: The Doctrine of Viewpoints claims there are seven ways of approaching an object of knowledge:

ONE: We may view the elephant simultaneously as an **individual being**, and as a **member of the elephant species**.

TWO: We may view the elephant merely as a **representative of the elephant species**, forgetting about any individual characteristics.

THREE: We may think of the elephant as purely an **individual elephant**, focusing on her personal traits and ignoring the fact that she is a member of a species.

FOUR: We may view the elephant as **existing in the present moment**, occupying a specific space.

FIVE: We might **contemplate the elephant in terms of the word "mammal,"** so that we do not misuse the word "mammal."

SIX: We may consider the elephant as a "mammal" in the **conventional** sense of the word, without probing into the history or etymology of the word "mammal."

SEVEN: Finally, we may view the elephant from the angle of the **etymology of the word "mammal."**

Alice: Well, what does a word mean?

WHEN I USE A WORD IT MEANS JUST WHAT I CHOOSE IT TO MEAN —

Humpty Dumpty: —neither more nor less. And that's exactly what the priestly Brahman class claimed. So, you can see, the Jain Doctrine of Many-sidedness pulled the rug out from under the sacred authority of the Vedas and the Brahman class.

Caterpillar: And the Jains were just the beginning of the Brahman's problems. A much bigger threat to Brahmanism was posed by a certain young prince.

Alice: A certain young prince?

BUDDHISM

Well, I'm getting a little ahead of myself. Let me set the scene. India has always been a land of extremes—famine and floods, asceticism and eroticism. The brutal heat of summer wilts and burns the vegetation, drying up fields, lakes, and swamplands. In the hot dust, water buffaloes shake their horns to drive away busy swarms of gnats from their bloodshot eyes.

In June, everything changes. The earth, parched and cracked open with the heat, suddenly begins to feel the cool balm of easterly monsoon breezes. Confused masses of clouds seethe on the horizon, building into mountainous thunderheads. The sky blackens, then opens with such devastating power that the pouring water seems solid rather than moving.

Nights are deep; thick clouds obscure the moon and stars, and the darkness seems even darker when interrupted by flashes of lightning. Five beautiful young women hurry through the downpour to meet their lover, a certain young prince, their thin rain-soaked saris clinging transparently to their breasts. Gathering them all into his arms, the prince makes love with them to the sound of the rumbling downpour and the accompaniment of 100 lovely court musician maidens. The riverbanks overflow, and schools of fish, bright as coins, dart over what yesterday was dust.

Unbeknown to the certain prince and his harem—in a distant forest, a yogi, thin as a bamboo reed, is sitting. The rainclouds have not yet reached him. He sits in the hot sun. Instead of embracing five lovers, he sits meditating in the center of five blazing fires, driving his five senses inward, his semen-energy drawn up his spine like a pure flame of rainbow arching high and dispassionately over coal-dark thunderclouds.

Alice: Who is this certain prince? And isn't there a middle path that lies between the extremes of making love with five women and barbecuing yourself between five fires?

Caterpillar: Well, actually, the certain young Prince entwined in love with his harem is none other than the future **Buddha**. And the path he taught was a **Middle Way** between hedonism and asceticism.

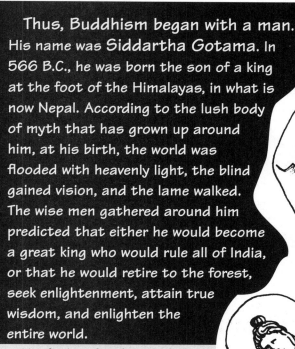

Thus, Buddhism began with a man. His name was **Siddartha Gotama**. In 566 B.C., he was born the son of a king at the foot of the Himalayas, in what is now Nepal. According to the lush body of myth that has grown up around him, at his birth, the world was flooded with heavenly light, the blind gained vision, and the lame walked. The wise men gathered around him predicted that either he would become a great king who would rule all of India, or that he would retire to the forest, seek enlightenment, attain true wisdom, and enlighten the entire world.

His father, fearful that the young Prince Gotama would become a spiritual seeker, provided him with the best worldly education, built him mansions as white as autumn clouds, gave him a sensuous wife, **Yashodara**, more beautiful than the Goddess of Beauty, hundreds of lovely maids to play him refined music in the cool evenings, and 40,000 dancing girls to entertain him with their charms.

Yet, although his father spared no effort to fill Prince Gotama's life with worldly pleasures and shield it from suffering, he was confined to the interior of his palaces. Of course, Gotama heard of various wonders which lay outside the palace walls: woods filled with birdsong, ponds brimming with blushing lotuses. The young prince began to feel like a caged elephant.

Hearing of this, his father arranged an excursion. Young Gotama was to tour the city. His father made sure that anyone old, sick, or dead should be cleared from the royal route. The young prince rode out. At first Gotama found the city a joyful paradise full of well-behaved, healthy citizens. But, according to legend, the Gods created, and placed three eyesores in his path: a broken-toothed old man, a man whose body was racked with disease, and a stinking corpse.

Deeply shocked at these sights, the young Gotama asked his charioteer if he, too, would suffer these afflictions. His charioteer replied, "Yes, you, too, shall suffer them."

The next sight the Prince saw was a wandering hermit with his begging bowl—the same hermit who had been barbecuing himself between the five fires. He looked happy and serene.

The young Gotama became pensive. He sat down beneath a Jambu tree, contemplated old age, sickness, and death, and decided to leave home. The voluptuous breasts, lilting lute melodies, and savory feasts that had surrounded him at the palace now only mocked him. He saw their transitory nature. In the dead of night he went back to the palace and stole into the bedroom of his dancing girls, where they lay sleeping. One beautiful woman lay with her sexual organs exposed, snoring loudly, her limbs all askew. Another lay with fixed eyes—their whites showing—resembling the corpse he had seen. Still another lay slobbering in her sleep, stinking, with spit drooling down her dream-distorted face. Disgusted, the young prince fled the palace.

He soon discovered that there were many hermits, sadhus, yogis, and ascetics wandering about northern India attempting to find release from the chains of worldly existence. This was, after all the Shramanic period. India was full of Jains and yogis, many of whom had rejected the authority of the Brahman priests and their sacrifices. What, after all, could these do for the average man? India, herself, was changing, becoming more urban. Old tribal structures were breaking down, and people were beginning to experience themselves as individuals in an urban environment. It was a somewhat insecure, but exciting, new world.

Siddartha Gotama became the student of two wandering Brahman ascetics. He learned all the highest meditation techniques of Hinduism. Despite all he had learned, however, he one day realized that neither of his teachers had gained a spiritual solution for human suffering. He went his own way.

Next, he joined a group of wandering Shramanas. For six years he practiced severe penance, fasting on six grains of rice a day, performing strenuous breathing exercises until he was blue in the face. He became so shriveled from fasting that his backbone protruded through his flesh. His skin became as tough as leather. He grew so weak that he could no longer meditate.

Suddenly, Siddartha Gotama had a realization. He had grown up surrounded by worldly pleasures. Then, he had gone to the other extreme, becoming a hermit who practiced strict asceticism. He became so weakened he could not even think straight. As a result, Gotama realized the need for a new type of path, a **Middle Path** or **Middle Way** between the extremes of worldly hedonism and asceticism.

Buddha: "O Monks, there are two extremes which should not be practiced by any person who has left society to find salvation. What are these extremes? On the one hand, there is the realm of desire and the pursuit of pleasure which is in accord with desire—it is a base pursuit, boorish, profane, crude, and without profit. On the other hand, there is the pursuit of self-mortification which is sheer misery, as well as crude and without profit. Monks, passing through these two extremes and avoiding them both is the Middle Way, object of the Buddha's perfect awakening, opening the eyes and the mind, leading to peace, to omniscience, to complete awakening, and to **Nirvana**."

Caterpillar: According to legend, just as he gained this realization, the daughter of a cow herder approached him, offering him a bowl of rice milk. He accepted the rice milk. His fellow hermits, however, abandoned him, because he had broken his fast.

Then, he sat with renewed strength beneath a tree, which came to be knows as the **Bo Tree**, the **Tree of Wisdom**. He vowed not to move until he was spiritually illumined.

The Mad Hatter: Of course, at this point the **Cosmic Tempter** came to disrupt his meditation, assuming the forms of voluptuous maidens dancing seductively before him; then transforming himself into powerful hurricanes, torrential rains, and flaming rocks. But these astral weapons only became a shower of flower petals as they entered Gotama's aura.

The Tempter next assaulted Gotama with his entire army, but Gotama touched the earth with one finger, and the earth thundered, scaring the evil army away.

On the night of a full moon in May, the Bo Tree began showering rosy petals. Gotama's meditation deepened until the morning star twinkled overhead, and Gotama entered perfect peace, becoming **Buddha**, the **Enlightened One**!

The entire universe trembled with delight! The earth and planets shuddered as if in love. The stars in the million galaxies quaked like petals in a breeze, so that the entire universe resembled garlands of fragrant white flowers whirling though the darkness of space.

The Buddha attempted to rise from the spot of his enlightenment, but wave after wave of bliss washed over him, and he was not able to leave his rapture until the 49th day. The Buddha was ready to go out and instruct the world in the Middle Way. But the Tempter appeared once more before him.

Tempter: Why try to teach your experience to un-comprehending idiots lost in seeking status and worldly pleasures? Why not just slip out of your body, ummmmmmm, into something more comfortable, like—Nirvana?

Buddha: Hmmmmm...tempting. But there will be some who will understand.

Alice: So. What was there to understand, if the Awakened one's experience was truly beyond words?

Caterpillar: In his first sermon, which he delivered in Deer Park in the town of Sarnath, he expounded his basic teaching—The Middle Way. It consists of the **Four Noble Truths** and the **Eight-fold Path**.

The Four Noble Truths
THE FIRST NOBLE TRUTH:
All life is *dukkha*. Life is a bummer. (***Dukkha*** is usually translated from Sanskrit as "suffering.")

Alice: How can Buddha claim that all life is suffering, when he is married to the most beautiful woman in the world and has 40,000 dancing girls?

Well, dukkha does not mean "suffering," exactly. The Buddha does not deny the fact that life can be filled with many plea-sures. But even rock stars who party with all the groupies they want end up spiritually frustrated, and sometimes even end up pulling the plug on themselves!
Dukkha is the awareness that birth is painful, old age is painful, sick-ness is painful, sorrow, grief, and despair are painful.
Not getting what you want is painful. Being stuck with what you don't want is painful. Even getting what you want is painful, when you realize that the joy is only transitory.

THE SECOND NOBLE TRUTH: *Dukkha* has a cause. This cause is thirsting—craving satisfaction and permanence in things that are impermanent, transitory, and elusive. Since everything is **transitory**, if we try to **make** things permanent, and **cling** to them, we suffer.

THE THIRD NOBLE TRUTH: *Dukkha* **can be abolished** by eliminating thirst or craving. This cessation of thirst is **Nirvana**.

THE FOURTH NOBLE TRUTH: The fourth noble truth tells us how we can accomplish the end of *dukkha* and the cessation of thirst. Anyone can do this by following the Eight-fold Path.

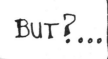

BUT?....

The Eight-fold Path

Alice: Wait a minute! That sounds like Patanjali's eight-limbed (ashtanga) yoga!

Caterpillar: That's right. Like Patanjali's eight-limbed yoga, the Eight-fold Path is not a sequence of steps, but rather the components of enlightenment, or Nirvana.

PERFECTED POINT OF VIEW: In other words, an understanding of the Four Noble Truths.

PERFECTED INTENTIONS: In the direction of non-attachment.

PERFECTED SPEECH: Speech free of malice, gossip, and negativity.

PERFECTED ACTION: Actions which produce only good vibes and good karma.

PERFECTED LIVELIHOOD: Avoidance of work harmful to others.

PERFECTED EFFORT: Setting forward the good.

PERFECTED MINDFULNESS: Mindfulness concerning the body, feelings, mind, and mental concepts.

PERFECTED CONCENTRATION: The state of samadhi.

The Four Noble Truths and the Eightfold Path, taken together, constitute the Middle Way of the Buddha.

Alice: Well, this sounds a whole lot like Hinduism to me! What's the big deal about Buddhism? What's the difference?

Caterpillar: **First:** Remember that Buddha appeared in the Shramanical period. Yet, unlike many of the Hindu and Jain Shramanas or strivers of that era, he finally gave up extreme forms of asceticism such as fasting. He dissed such excessive striving in favor of a Middle Way that falls between the extremes of sensual dalliance with 1,000 concubines and sitting on a bed of nails!

Second: The Buddha's teaching about individual experience and the nature of the world was a radical departure from the Hindu and Jain perspectives. Whereas the Hindus and Jains believed in **things**, the Buddha did not. The Hindus and Jains conceived of the universe in terms of two super big things: a spiritual Self (**Atman, jiva, purusha**) and its relationship to a Not-Self (**maya, a-jiva, prakriti**).

Buddha, on the other hand, philosophized that neither the "Self" nor the "World," neither *jiva* nor *a-jiva*, are substantial things at all. They are only insubstantial, phantasmagoric, dream-like events-processes. Concepts such as the Atman or Self are just the inventions of language. Instead of talking about the "Self" and the "Not-Self," the Buddhists talk about their own concept: the **No-Self** (**An-Atman**)!

Third: Buddha did not accept any authority, especially the supposed authority of the Vedas or of the priestly Brahman class. For Buddha, the Vedas were not the eternal Word at the basis of creation. Words, even Vedic words, are just arbitrary and conventional. According to the Buddha, teachers of the Veda are just like the blind leading the blind. He felt everyone should be their own authority, working out their own salvation for themselves.

Fourth: Buddha did not follow traditions. Therefore, he taught in Prakrit, the common language of the people, rather than in Sanskrit, the elitist language of the Brahman priests.

Fifth: Buddha's teaching was psychological rather than religious. It aimed at conquering the psychological barrier of craving or desire—not in kissing up to the Gods of the Vedic universe. Buddhism concerns itself with human reality rather than divine reality.

Sixth: Buddha was egalitarian. Hindus taught that only Brahmans could reach enlightenment, whereas Buddha taught that enlightenment was equally available to every human being. Buddha also rejected the caste system.

Seventh: The Buddha rejected the excessive ritualism of the Hindus, especially the Vedic rituals or **yagyas**. He argued that the rituals were ineffectual, because the Gods they were directed towards were mere fictions. For Buddha, the belief in yagyas was one of the main obstacles to true spirituality.

Eighth: Buddha refused to indulge in metaphysical discussions. To ask whether the world is eternal or noneternal, or whether or not reincarnation exists, for example, were questions he refused to quibble over. He felt such debates are a waste of time.

Alice: What did the Buddha do after his enlightenment?

Caterpillar: He wandered all over the Eastern Ganges valley organizing and teaching his monastic community. Yet, because he himself was of royal lineage, he was also able to befriend and instruct kings and other wealthy patrons who provided the monks with their daily needs. He died at the age of 80.

The band of monks Buddha left behind continued to develop and spread his teachings. They received a lot of help from **Ashoka**, an Indian emperor in the 3rd century B.C., who converted to Buddhism, and united all of India.

Though he was Buddhist, his *Edicts*, which were carved on rocks, pillars, and the walls of caves, taught religious tolerance. But the early Buddhist monks also began to argue among themselves about the true teachings of the Buddha. This, of course, led to a schism.

The Big Raft and The Little Raft

Caterpillar: On the one side of the divide were the **Theravada Buddhists**. **Theravada** means "The Way of the Elders." They felt their way was the closest to the true teaching of Buddha. Their rivals called themselves **Mahayana**, or **Big Raft, Buddhists**, and called the Theravadins somewhat sarcastically, **Hinayana** (**Little Raft**) **Buddhists**. Their rivalry, throughout history, has often been as heated as those between surfers who surf long boards and those who surf short boards.

THERAVADA (LITTLE RAFT)

1. Buddha was a saint.
2. Individual salvation based on wisdom is the goal.
3. Real enlightenment is not for sissies. One should work at it full-time. Therefore, you need to be a monk and belong to a **sangha** or community.
4. Our hero is the **Arhat**, who seeks Nirvana for himself.
5. Metaphysical speculation is a waste of time.
6. Meditation is the way!
7. There is only one Buddha who was the founder of Buddhism.
8. We teach only the original **Pali Canon**, in Prakrit language.
9. Everything is just a collection of elements (**dharmas**) which are always in flux.
10. Come join us in Sri Lanka, Thailand, Burma, Cambodia, and Laos.

MAHAYANA (BIG RAFT)

1. Buddha was a savior.
2. Compassion for others is important. Seek enlightenment for oneself, but also for others.
3. Enlightenment is a path not just for monks, but for all people.
4. Our hero is the **Bodhisattva**, who on the edge of Nirvana, pulls back so that he can bring the rest of the world to Nirvana also.
5. **Au contraire**! There are 37 Buddhist Hells and 53 Heavens!
6. Prayers to Buddha are answered! We also indulge in rituals!
7. Everyone has a Buddha nature, and can become a Buddha.
8. We teach many other scriptures, many of them in Sanskrit.
9. All things are Empty (**shunyata**).
10. Come join us in China, Korea, Tibet, Mongolia, Nepal, and Vietnam.

Whereas the Theravadins believed the world to be made up of very small things, continually in flux, the Mahayanins believed that all things were Empty.
Alice: Empty?

Madhyamika Buddhism

Caterpillar: The founder of this doctrine of Emptiness was **Nagarjuna**, and his particular school of Buddhism was known as **Madhyamika Buddhism**. Madhyamika means "The Middle Path." It is a radical abandonment of the Hindu and Jain obsessions with a metaphysical, transcendental Absolute.

During Nagarjuna's era, which was sometime between the 1st and 2nd centuries A.D., many schools of Buddhism were flowering. They debated not only among themselves but with Hindu and Jain philosophers as well.

After Plato's academy in Athens, Nalanda was the second university in the entire history of the planet. It gained an international reputation, drawing scholars from afar, and became a hive of intellectual debate, where some made lean matters fat, and others made fat matters lean, where sagacious debaters ripped apart their opponents' hypotheses, arguments, and conclusions as vultures tear apart a morsel of raw meat tossed into the air, where Hindus, Jains, Buddhist, materialists, Chinese Taoists, and Persian and Greek philosophers all argued their positions with force and subtlety.

Among this cacophony of contending theories arose the thought of Nagarjuna, sometimes called "The Second Buddha." After Buddha, he was the greatest Buddhist philosopher, and the most influential philosopher in all of Asian history. His thought, which provided the basis for Mahayana philosophy, influenced many schools of Buddhist philosophy, including **Zen**. He also had an influence on Hindu and Taoist philosophy.

We know little of Nagarjuna's life, other than the fact that he grew up on the balmy, palm, fringed coast of southern India, and spent much of his life there. Legend has it that he was a magician, and also a playboy. In fact one night, it is said, that while the full moon was floating overhead, a night alive with clapping hands, throbbing drums, and the hum of sitars, a night perfumed with the rich odors of wines and dark clouds of incense, Nagarjuna was lost somewhere between the tinkling anklets and sandalwood-scented breasts of his local raja's harem.

The tinkling of the little bells on their anklets and bracelets mingled with their sighs and laughter, the motions of their swimming hips, their floating veils, their slender, entwined, trembling limbs, their pleasure-flooded, wide swooning eyes. . . It was not until their passion was spent, and there remained nothing but a sea of slumbering beauties, with Nagarjuna dreamily adrift somewhere in their center, that they were discovered by the royal guards.

Nagarjuna felt so guilty about this incident that he embraced a new way of life: Buddhist monkhood. The boob-deprived youth then came up with an appropriate concept—**Emptiness**. He thus became Asia's most influential philosopher.

He writes about Emptiness in the *Mulamadhyamakakarika* (*Verses on the Authentic Middle Way*). According to myth, Nagarjuna did not write this scripture himself. It was given to him when he dived deep into the sea to the home of a Serpent King.

Nagarjuna delivered a brilliant sermon on Buddhism, which so delighted the Serpent King that he gave Nagarjuna a whole library of scriptures, telling Nagarjuna that they were the authentic words of the Buddha!

Alice: What is Emptiness?

The Mad Hatter: Well, anything that is Empty is devoid of **self-essence**. Or in Sanskrit what is called **svabhava**.

Alice: Self-essence?

The Mad Hatter: You see this cup?

It seems to exist all by itself, and not to be dependent on, or related to, anything else. But is this a drawing of a cup or of two faces? Or is it a drawing of both, or of neither? Perhaps it is just a two-dimensional series of lines!

Alice: Perhaps it is all of these things, or none of them!

The Mad Hatter: The important point is that we cannot see both the cup and the faces simultaneously. Each image appears to possess svabhava or self-essence. Each image appears to be a self-sufficient, self-existent, discrete image.

Alice: But they **don't** possess self-essence! There is an intimate, subtle relationship between the faces and the cup. One cannot exist without the other. They **depend** on each other.

The Mad Hatter: According to Nagarjuna, we tend to think in terms of such dichotomies. For instance, we have seen that the Hindus and Jains thought the universe is made up of this pair:

1 **An eternal spiritual Self (which possesses svabhava)**
2 **and a Non-Self, made up of Matter.**

This fundamental dichotomy lies at the basis of all Hindu and Jain experience.

But the Buddhist will say that **neither** the Self **nor** the Non-Self are substantial.

Likewise, a fundamentalist Christian or Muslim will claim that only his religion is true, and that every other religion is myth or of the devil. We tend to form these dichotomies and to favor one member of the pair. Either Christian or Muslim.

But the cup and the faces are not separate. Each image is in a subtle and intimate relationship with its hidden partner.

58

Though they cannot be seen at the same time, neither of them exists alone. Neither of them possesses svabhava or self-existence. In fact you could say that they are Empty of self-existence. This does not mean that they don't exist, that they don't appear. Emptiness just means that the illusion of their separateness is a mirage.

Let's not forget, Nagarjuna was a magician who often used the metaphor of magic to illustrate his points:

Suppose, for instance, a magician, by means of magic, transforms my harem into an elephant! Both the magician and his audience see the same elephant! It looks to both of them just like an elephant. But only the audience really believes it really is an elephant. Only the audience wants to go for an elephant ride. To the magician, the elephant is an illusion.

But to a man in the audience, eating peanuts, it makes sense to say "I want to give it my nuts! I want to go for a ride!"

Ordinary people are like the magician's audience. They assume that everything has self-existence. They become emotionally and intellectually attached to the "things" they perceive. Thus, most people only see the ordinary level of truth (**samvritisatya**).

Those who see the Emptiness of things are like the magician—he sees the same things, but from a different point of view. He knows that things are empty of a fixed self-existent nature. He simply perceives things accurately. Thus he sees the Ultimate level of truth (paramarthasatya).

And even the concept of these two levels of truth is Empty of self-existence! For if you cling to the concept of Ultimate Truth, then it becomes the Lower Conventional Truth!

Alice: Awesome! Can you explain more about the two levels of truth?

The Mad Hatter: Suppose you look into a looking glass, and you see your own image—but you think that it is the real (unreflected) Alice.

Alice: Okay.

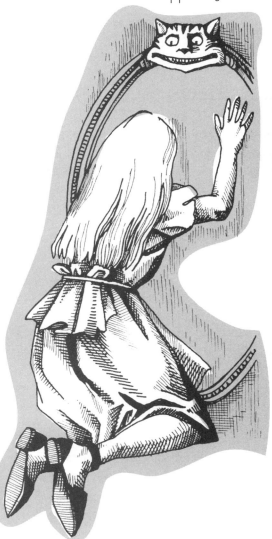

The Mad Hatter: But then you suddenly realize that the reflection is not what it appears to be.

Alice: Okay.

The Mad Hatter: This does not mean the reflection does not exist. The reflection now seems to be an **illusion** only because you **had** believed it was the **real** you. But **now** you know that the reflection in the looking glass does **not** have self-existence. After all, the reflection depends upon the mirror, the eyes and mind of the real Alice, etc.

But this doesn't mean that you simply abandon the reflection. It is still useful to you for combing your hair, etc. The reflection is like the **Lower Conventional Truth**. Realizing it is only a reflection devoid of self-existence is like the **Higher Truth**. According to Nagarjuna, everything in the world is like the reflection in the mirror.

The Mad Hatter: One needs to avoid extreme dualisms. One way to do this is through the concept of **dependent arising** (***pratityasamutpadah***). For instance, this tea does not have self-existence, because it is a dependent arising.

Alice: Arising?

The Mad Hatter: Yes. It is here before your vision, it has "arisen." But the tea is dependent on the sun and rains that helped it grow, upon the pickers who picked it, upon the earth in which it grew. . . in short, it is dependent on many other dependent arisings.

When you understand that the tea is dependent upon them, you eliminate the extreme view that it is self-existent.

And when you understand that the tea is an arising, you avoid the extreme position that it doesn't exist.

Alice: So by acknowledging that the tea is a dependent arising I avoid both extremes: that the tea possesses self-existence, and that it doesn't even exist at all.

The Mad Hatter: Yes. Another tool Nagarjuna uses is the **tetra-lemma** or *Catuskoti*?

Suppose you are experiencing fear. To apply the tetra-lemma to your emotion of fear, you ask the fear four questions:

1 Is this fear producing itself?

(Does it have self-existence?) The answer is no, because nothing can produce itself. Nothing has self-existence.

2 Is this fear produced by some other self-existing thing?

No, this is also impossible, because we have just said that nothing has self-existence. Therefore the fear cannot be produced by anything else.

3 Is the fear caused by both?

No, it cannot be. This is impossible. Because how can both produce it if neither can?

4 Is this fear produced by neither itself nor by anything else?

No, because then it would be produced by nothing.

HEEEEEEERE'S JACQUIE!

Alice: Well then, if the fear cannot be produced by anything, if I cannot analytically find this fear, what happens to it?

The Mad Hatter: Its loses its force. Actually, it disappears. It has been deconstructed. In fact many authors have written about the similarities between Nagarjuna's thought and that of the French Moroccan philosopher **Jacques Derrida** (See *Derrida for Beginners* and *Postmodernism for Beginners*).

One difference between Derrida's "**deconstruction**" and Madhya-mika is that people who deconstruct usually deconstruct "things" like books, laws, and institutions. Buddhists, however, use Empti-ness to deal with their own emotional life, and gain enlightenment.

Alice: So is Emptiness a thing?

The Mad Hatter: No. That would be like a shopkeeper who says, "I have nothing to sell you!" And then the customer replies, "Very well, then, just sell me some of that nothing."

In fact, Madhyamika, like deconstruction, is a kind of **non-posi-tion**, a **non-philosophy**, for it asserts **no thing**, it makes **no claims**. Like both Chinese and Japanese Zen, which it made possible, it is **non-metaphysical** and only deconstructs the metaphysical preten-sions of other philosophies.

Yogachara Buddhism

The Mad Hatter: A second great school of Indian Buddhism is the **Yogachara** (**Practice of Meditation**) **School**. It is also known as the *Vijnanavada* (**Doctrine of Consciousness**) **School**. Founded by the poet, logician, and philosopher **Vasubandu** and his half-brother **Asanga**, the school teaches that everything we perceive exists only in our consciousness. A tree, a galaxy, an elephant, these are nothing more than mental projections.

Alice: But if we both go to see *Gone With the Wind*, we both see *Gone with the Wind*—so the movie must exist externally to us.

The Mad Hatter: Well, that's because we have a similar storehouse of impressions (**alayavijnana**) from our past actions (**karma**). Beings who have similar impressions stored in their mental storehouse see similar things. A fish would not see *Gone with the Wind* in the same way. Similarly, all the demons people see in Hell are just communal projections—not real demons. It is just a group fantasy the people in Hell imagine in order to torture themselves. And they are all only in Hell and being tortured by the demons because of their karma.

TARA?

Alice: But every human who sees *Gone with the Wind* sees *Gone with the Wind*.

The Mad Hatter: Well, perhaps that is one of the faults of this system.

But there is one thing that is free of human thought. This is called **Tathata**, or **Suchness**. The way to achieve Suchness is to purify the storehouse of impressions until it becomes like pure being itself. The way to do this is through yoga and meditation practice in which you learn to **visualize**.

For instance, if you visualize that you have become an elephant, you will begin to realize that your vision seems just as real as "real" perceptions. Then you will realize that all things are subjective. Like the Madhyamika school, they felt that all things were empty of self-existence. But unlike the Madhyamikins, they believed that there is a thought process, or thinking mind, behind all things.

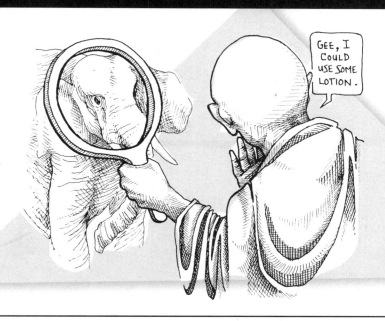

GEE, I COULD USE SOME LOTION.

This is why the school is sometimes called the **Mind Only** or **Consciousness Only** School. After Vasubandhu, a series of teachers developed **Yogacharya**. At Nalanda, the famous university, **Hsuan-tsang**, a visiting Chinese scholar, learned Yogacharya, and took the teaching back to China.

We have seen that the Shramanical Hindus, Jains, and Buddhists rebelled against the Indo-Brahmanical practices of ritual sacrifice and priestly authority. Yet another reaction that began to develop during this period is the cults of worship (**bhakti**) of personal deities such as **Shiva**, **Vishnu**, and **the Goddess**. **Pujas**, or rituals of personal devotion, replaced the complex and expensive Vedic yagyas which tried to mechanically manipulate the Gods. Worship of a personal God or Goddess would play a prominent role in the next period.

THE INDIC TRUNK (c. 300-1200 A.D.)

This is also commonly called the **Classical Hindu Period.** It is a misleading name, however, because Hindu, Buddhist, and Jain thought were in a constant hairsplitting philosophical and cultural dialogue. Hinduism did not refute or reject Buddhism, Jainism, and Shramanical ascetic tendencies, but devoured them, making them a part of Hinduism's own body. Religiously, Hinduism flowered during this period, blending elements from the ancient Indus Valley culture, from the Indo-Brahmanical traditions, and from the ascetic yogic practices of the Indo-Shramanical period.

Bhakti

Whereas the religion of the Vedic rituals was mainly for the wealthy and the priests, and the cult of yoga was mostly for monks, **bhakti** was for the common people. Bhakti means "devotion," and is more concerned with emotions like **love** than with knowledge or power.

Alice: How did the bhaktis worship?

Instead of sacrificing horses to the Gods of the Vedas with Vedic yagyas, or sacrifices, the people of this period began to worship their own chosen Gods and Goddesses with hibiscus flowers, incense, water, milk, ghee, and other offerings. The puja is a much more personal form of worship than the yagya. It involves devotional singing, dancing, and image worship.

Alice: Well, then, who did they worship?

Caterpillar: The main Gods of this period are **Brahma** (**The Creator**), **Vishnu** (**The Maintainer**), and **Shiva** (**The Destroyer**).

Alice: The Destroyer! Shiva sounds cool. What does he destroy?

Caterpillar: Shiva is a dancer with a tangle of wild, matted dreadlocks tangled like snakes that whirl when he dances like a whirlpool. He dances out the terrible act of world destruction. He dances with a trident in one hand, and his fiery eyes, beard, and hair shine like a mountain summit garlanded by forest fires! His wild laughter reverberates deeply like thundering monsoon clouds. The wind whistles and howls within the hollows of his necklace of skulls, tossing with the incessant rhythm of his dance. The hurricane of his whirling, dancing limbs destroys the world.

Alice: Awesome!

But he is also the best yogi in the universe. His poetry is the four Vedas. He has three eyes, his body is smeared with ashes, and in his hair he wears the crescent moon dripping with cool blissful nectar. The stream of the Ganga (Ganges) River pours from his crown, wherein the moon, like a silver minnow, dives and surfaces.

He sits in the cross-legged full lotus posture, each sense subdued by meditation. He sits straight and tall with his hands lying in his lap, palms up, like a blossomed lotus, with a snake tying up the matted mass of his hair, **rudraksha** beads in double strings hanging from his ears, wearing the skin of a black antelope. He is still. His vision is turned inward. His wild pupils are stilled, with changeless eyebrows, with unquivering lashes, his mind like a body of water without any waves. With breath stopped, he sees with absolute vision the calm eternity of the Self within the Self.

Alice: Awesome!

Caterpillar: Yet, he is also the world's greatest lover. His lover is the Goddess **Uma, The Golden One.** Bending a little from the weight of her own breasts, her skin the color of the young sun, she resembles a budding vine curved down by its thick clusters of flowers. Uma kisses Shiva. Shiva hugs Uma. Uma's breasts melt into each other. Uma melts into Shiva. Shiva melts into the Self. Consciousness melts into Consciousness.

Alice: Awesome! But who, then, is **Vishnu**?

Caterpillar: Whereas **Brahma** creates the universe, and **Shiva** destroys it, **Vishnu** is **The Maintainer**. He is dark blue-black, the color of monsoon clouds. He is both the transcendent Self and the manifest world. He is the pillar of the universe, sustaining it. He has four arms. In one he holds a conch, in another a discus, in the third a mace, and in the last a lotus flower. He has 10 incarnations: Fish, Tortoise, Boar, Dwarf, Man-Lion, a Warrior, **Rama**, **Krishna**, and Buddha. The future incarnation will be **Kalkin**, who rides a white horse.

Alice: Buddha was an incarnation of the God Vishnu?

Caterpillar: Well, according to the Hindu view of things. In fact, the Hindus basically kicked Buddhism out of India, but they also assimilated much of Buddhist philosophy and made the Buddha himself into a domesticated incarnation of Vishnu.

Vishnu is most often worshipped in his incarnations as **Krishna** and **Rama**. Rama is the hero of a great epic written by the poet **Valmiki**. This epic, known as the *Ramayana*, is the romance of an exiled prince whose princess, **Sita**, has been carried off by the demon **Ravana**. With the help of **Hanuman**, a magical monkey, Rama wages war against Ravana, and wins back Sita. The movie *Star Wars* is based on the *Ramayana*.

Krishna, the blue-black incarnation of Vishnu, plays an important role in the best known book in India, *The Bhagavad Gita*. Krishna is the charioteer of the Great archer **Arjuna**. Arjuna, however, seeing his own kinsmen and teachers in the opposing army, lays down his bow and refuses to fight. He is torn between the feelings of his heart, and his duty as a warrior. Krishna tells him to fight. Because it is not he, Arjuna, who kills, but Krishna himself. Moreover, what is killed is only the mortal body, and the soul is immortal and imperishable.

Alice: Well, what about Brahma, The Creator?

Caterpillar: Brahma? With mantras, the Hindus worship Brahma, the Lord of the Word, the Creator of All, with four faces—one facing each direction. Unborn, never knowing birth, he gives birth to the entire universe of forms, womb of the universe, born of no womb, the beginning of the universe, though he is without beginning, Lord of the universe, though he has no Lord, he knows Himself, and in knowing Himself, creates Himself, and by the power of His own Self, dissolves into Himself alone!

YONI — A REPRESENTATION OF THE FEMALE PRINCIPLE

Alice: He sounds a little narcissistic. Is he a popular fellow?

Caterpillar: Funny you should ask. In all of India he has only one temple remaining. This is because Hindus are more comfortable with the idea of a Goddess being the womb of the universe than a God serving that function. Hindus tend to worship **Mahadevi, The Great Goddess**, as the womb of the universe.

Alice: So the Hindus worship goddesses also?

Caterpillar: She is worshipped in three main forms: as **Kali**, as **Devi,** and as **Durga**. In fact, since pre-historic times, probably even before the Aryans invaded India, she has been worshipped with flowers, incense, etc. Archaeologists have unearthed female figurines and phallic objects that provide strong evidence of goddess worship in the Indus Valley civilization. During the Vedic period, the goddess worship was probably suppressed by the patriarchal Aryans. But in the Indic period, the pre-Aryan Goddess reemerged as wives of the Hindu Gods. The wife of Brahma is **Saraswati.** The wife of Vishnu is **Lakshmi**. And the wife of Shiva is **Parvati.** Saraswati and Lakshmi are little more than ornaments of their divine spouses. Their male spouses come first, and their role is to support them. Only Shiva's wife, Parvati, is an erotic THANG all her own, celebrated in poetry, myth, and ritual.

YONI AND LINGAM— MALE AND FEMALE CONJOINED

Shiva's wife and lover also goes by the name of **Shakti,** which means "energy" or "power." Her devotees call themselves **Shaktas,** as they worship the "power" that creates and sustains the world, and destroys demonic forces. Their holy books are called *Tantras,* or esoteric manuals, full of sexual symbolism. They praise the feminine principle of the universe and the importance of the physical body in gaining enlightenment.

Shiva is not absent from the **Tantric** traditions. He is Pure Consciousness, eternally inactive, at the basis of the universe. He cannot act and manifest without Shakti, his lover, his "power." Shakti is creative energy.

Her most popular form is **Durga, The Hard to Approach.** Supremely beautiful, dripping with blood, she is a fierce lover of war and is insatiably cruel, pulverizing and devouring her enemies without mercy. She straddles a lion and rides him into battle, her 20 arms wielding tridents, bows, arrows, swords, daggers, snakes, and other weapons.

Alice: What a bitch!

Caterpillar: Yet she is a tender mother, protecting all those who ask her for shelter.

But she has an even more terrible form: as **Kali.** Kali's skin is inky-black with rage. She has a hideous, bloodthirsty face, and a necklace of snakes strung with severed human heads and skulls.

71

Alice: So if the Goddess displays all these forms, she is both benign and terrible, a destroyer and a nourisher.

Caterpillar: Tantric yogis meditate on **mantras**, which are the sonic forms of the Goddess. Every Goddess has a **bija mantra** or **seed mantra**, which is their body of sound.

In **Kundalini yoga**, a kind of Tantric practice, worship takes place within the devotee's own body—or rather within her subtle body. Kundalini means "coiled up." The divine Goddess Kundalini shines like the stem of a young lotus, like a snake coiled round upon herself, holding her tail in her mouth. She lies resting half asleep at the base of the spine.

Esoteric Tantric drawings depict a fine spiritual channel running from the base of the spine to the crown of the head. Along this path, known as the **sushumna,** *seven* **chakras** *or "wheels" of spiritual energy each contain certain Gods and Goddesses. In Kundalini yoga, the Goddess named Kundalini rises up through the sushumna, piercing and awakening one after another of the seven chakras. They blossom like lotuses at the touch of her divine energy. When she reaches the top chakra, the Thousand Petaled Lotus, above the crown of the head, the devotee is fully enlightened. Those who practice Kundalini yoga awaken the subtle kundalini energy through breath control, meditation, and sometimes through ritual sexual union.*

During the Indic period, Hindus, Jains, and Buddhists all believed in the idea of karma—that the seeds we sow, we shall reap. In fact, it is our own karma that makes us reincarnate, in the endless cycle of birth, death, and rebirth known as **samsara**. Just as a caterpillar that has reached the tip of a blade of grass draws itself together, and then stretches to reach a new blade, the individual soul, as death nears, gathers up its impressions, and then, leaving the body, reaches out towards a new one.

If you are lucky enough to obtain a human body, then through disciplined meditation, and the various paths of yoga based on love, knowledge, or good works, you can free yourself from the effects of karma, and gain release from rebirth, samsara. You can gain enlightenment!

Alice: But what about everyday life? I mean, not everyone can just sit around doing yoga all day!

Caterpillar: Hinduism is not just a collection of philosophies and texts and religious practices, but a way of life that determines every daily action from getting married to going to the bathroom. If you are a Hindu, everything you do is subject to many rules and regulations. These rules and regulations are collected in a group of texts called the **Dharma Shastras** or **Law Books**. These books list the four purposes of human life, the **four stages** of human life, and the four **castes**.

The Four Aims of Life

1 **KAMA.** *Kama* embraces the realm of pleasures and desires: reading and writing poetry, painting, and erotic dalliance.

2 **ARTHA.** *Artha* means "wealth" or "work." Most of us, after all, have to work at a career in order to play.

3 **DHARMA.** *Dharma* means "duty" or "law," and includes all the rules of social behavior in our community.

4 **MOKSHA.** *Moksha* means "liberation" or "release."

Caterpillar: Suppose that every night, you have probed every sexual position in the *Kama Sutra* with a different lover. And suppose you have worked during the days, becoming a business tycoon worth a fortune. Suppose you are a respectable member of the community, an honorary chairperson of 20 different societies and charitable institutions, a speaker at funerals and unveiling ceremonies, and that there is a bronze statue of you astride a stallion in every major park in every major city on every major planet. But still, you don't feel fulfilled! You ask, "Is there anything else?"

REAL LIFE? SHEESH I'M TOO EXHAUSTED.

This is the moment moksha has been waiting for. And it answers with a resounding "yes." Moksha is real life, it is infinite bliss, being, and consciousness. Open your awareness to the glory of your own inner Self, and attain enlightenment! Gain release from birth, death, and rebirth! This is moksha.

Alice: But then, what are the Four Stages of Life?

THE FOUR STAGES OF LIFE

Caterpillar: The Four Stages of Life are known as the four **ashramas**. They are:

Brahmacharin: Once a child reaches between the ages 8 and 12, he is initiated, and then moves into the house of his teacher or guru, where he lives for 12 years, studying one-pointedly in celibacy.

> "Let an Aryan youth dwell in the house of his teacher. Let him study the Vedas, and offer libations of water to the Gods and sages. Let him abstain from meat, honey, perfumes, garlands, women, fermented foods, and doing injury to living creatures."

Grihastya: After completing his education, it is time for the young man to enter the second stage of life: that of the householder. Usually his parents consult with an astrologer and arrange for his marriage. During this stage he performs all his family and community duties, gains material wealth, and enjoys life as a husband, lover, and father. The householder is very important in Hindu society because he financially supports the other three stages.

> "As all rivers, both great and small, find a resting place in the ocean, even so men of all stages of life find protection with householders."

Vanaprasthya: During the third stage of life, an elderly couple can set up a home in the forest, retire, and devote themselves to the attainment of enlightenment, or moksha.

> "When a householder sees his skin wrinkled, and his hair white, and the sons of his sons, then he may resort to the forest."

Samnyasa: Ideally, in the final stage of life, the seeker enters into an even more radical form of renunciation, becoming a homeless, naked, wandering ascetic in pursuit of moksha. He wanders naked, like a wild swan that migrates from the snow-capped Himalayas to the sunny south of India with the seasons.

"By deep meditation, let him recognize the subtle nature of the supreme Self, and its presence in all organisms. . ."

Alice: And what about the four castes?

THE FOUR CASTES

Caterpillar: The entire caste system is based on the Veda. Originally caste distinctions were very fluid. They only became rigid during the Indo-Islamic period.

The caste system is like a huge pyramid, with the Brahman priests on top:

1 The highest caste is the **Brahmans** or priests, performers of rituals and learned in the sacred texts called the Vedas.

"Teaching, studying, sacrificing for himself, sacrificing for others, making gifts, and receiving them, are the six acts prescribed for a Brahman."

2 The next highest caste is the **Kshatriya** or warrior class. These families are responsible for governing, kingship, and military service.

"A Kshatriya must protect the whole world!"

3 Go to any outdoor bazaar in India, and you will see members of the **Vaishya** class, knowledgeable in the value of pearls, coral, metals, cloth, perfumes, and spices such as cumin, ginger, and

coriander. A savvy judge of the excellencies and defects of commodities, and shrewd in the knowledge of how to turn a profit, a Vaishya is versed in the various languages and dialects of men with whom he might trade.

4 The lowest class is that of the **Shudras**: servants, or unskilled laborers.

"To serve Brahmans who are learned in the Vedas, householders famous for their virtuous acts, is the highest duty of a Shudra. His service leads to beatitude."

But there is still a lower caste, "the untouchables" or **Asprishyas**. Families whose occupations bring them into contact with human excrement, corpses, and the like—and who are thus considered unclean, are segregated from the castes considered to be purer and higher.

Alice: But what about women?

Manu: "Women must be honored and adored by their fathers, brothers, husbands, and brothers-in-law, who desire their own welfare. Where women are honored, there the Gods are pleased; but where they are not honored, no sacred rite yields rewards."

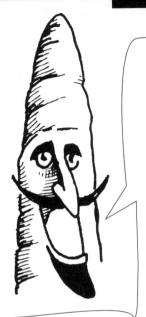

It was also during the Indic Era that illumined teachers formulated the **Six Classical Systems of Indian Philosophy**. These teachers tended to be monks, hermits, recluses, and ascetics, and wrote their teachings in concise verses called **sutras** or **karikas**. These philosophies or **Darshanas** (literally "points of view"), were not passed down as scriptures so much as they were transmitted by illumined gurus who had realized the truth of the teaching, and imparted its spiritual essence to their students. All six systems accept the authority of the Vedas. And all six share many common technical terms, though they each give different meanings to those terms. Each system is concerned with how to gain true knowledge. Intuition is usually given the highest place, with reason subordinate to intuition. All the systems react to the skeptical tone of Buddhist philosophy. All the systems hold in common the great cosmic cycles of time. And most of them are concerned with enlightenment.

Alice: But where did the six systems come from?

Caterpillar: Remember that the Vedas are made up of divine poetry. But the Buddha attacked the Vedas with cold logic. Therefore, the Hindus felt the need to defend their tradition, **logically**.

Nyaya

Caterpillar: It is no accident then, that the first school of Indian philosophy is **Nyaya**, the **science of how to come to conclusions through right or just reasoning**. It lays out the correct approach to an object of knowledge, and the correct means of gaining knowledge.

Of these **intuition** or direct perception is the highest method. Next is **inference**, which includes both deductive and inductive logic. Next is **comparison**. Last is **verbal testimony** from a trustworthy authority.

There are five parts to Nyaya logic:

THE HYPOTHESIS: This is an elephant I am touching.

THE REASON: Because I feel the dual curves of its frontal mounds.

THE EXAMPLE: Where there are frontal mounds, there is an elephant.

THE APPLICATION: This thing I am touching has frontal mounds.

THE CONCLUSION: Therefore, this is an elephant I am touching.

Nyaya inference depends upon a universal connection: for example, frontal mounds are universally connected (in India) with elephants.

Alice: Oh! I can see why **direct perception** is more accurate than **logical inference**!

Vaisheshika

Caterpillar: **Vaisheshika** is the second school. It is an **atomist philosophy** that teaches that reality is made up of a lot of little units: atoms. These do not arise from one common spiritual source, but are separate. Vaisheshika means "particularity"—and is both a system of physics and of metaphysics. The physical universe is made up of four types of atoms (**anu**): earthy ones, watery ones, fiery ones, and airy ones.

Vaisheshika reasons that the soul must exist, because consciousness cannot be dependent on the sense organs, body, or mind. Although **Kanada**, the author of the *Vaisheshika Sutra*, does not mention a God, later Nyaya philosophers believed that atoms could not intelligently arrange themselves into things like elephants and women without some sort of God.

Sankhya

The third school is **Sankhya**, or "enumeration." Sankhya's great teachers, **Kapila** and **Ishvarakrishna**, taught that we live in a dualistic world made up of **Primordial Matter** (**Prakriti**) and **Spirit** (**Purusha**). These are both real and separate. But when they interact, manifestation takes place in a certain (enumerated) sequence.

The first level of manifestation is **Buddhi** or **Intellect**. This is followed by **Ahamkara, I-making**, or the **Ego**. Then arises **Manas**, or **Mind**. Next appear the **five senses** and the **five powers of action**, movement, grasping, procreation, excretion. Then the elements of the physical universe arise: ether, air, fire, water, earth.

Pervading all of Prakriti, or Matter, are the **three gunas: rajas**, **tamas**, and **sattva**. Rajas is active. It is the guy in the red sports car who eats chili peppers. Sattva is pure. It is the illumined yogi in meditation who drinks milk. And tamas is dull. It is the diseased cancer victim who eats meat.

Yet, the individual is not the body or the mind. So the individual is not made up of the three gunas. The individual is really the silent, eternal, peaceful Self, the **Purusha**.

In the unenlightened person, the Purusha, or Self, gets mixed up with all the stuff of Prakriti, or Matter.

In the enlightened person, the Self stands apart, like oil and water. The way to gain liberation in **Sankhya** is through knowledge.

Yoga

Yoga is the fourth school of Indian philosophy. The Yoga system teaches the practical way to realize that Purusha is separate from Matter. Yoga was formally formulated by Patanjali, and has been discussed earlier. However, its roots may reach much deeper in history.

Mimamsa

Mimamsa is the fifth school. Mimamsa teaches that the only true source of knowledge is the Vedas. The rituals prescribed in the Vedas are the means of getting to Heaven.

Vedanta

Vedanta is the philosophy of Oneness. It is developed in the **Upanishads**. Vedanta means "the end of the Veda"! It elaborates the spiritual and philosophical thought of the Upanishads. The **Vedanta Sutras**, also called the **Brahma Sutra**, discuss the nature of Brahman, the highest reality. Because the sutras consists of only two or three words each, they need a commentary. The three main commentators were **Shankara**, **Ramanuja**, and **Madhva**.

Shankara (788-822 A.D.) is head guru of non-dualistic (**advaita**) Vedanta.

Alice: Advaita? Non-dualistic? What does this mean?

Caterpillar: It means that there is only one thing in the universe. Reality is One. Brahman is non-dual.

Alice: But how about all the things in the world? Don't they exist?

Caterpillar: They only exist through **ignorance**. Suppose you see a bunch of women. But you don't think it is a bunch of women, you think it is an elephant! So you pray that the elephant will not trample your watermelons. But your action and knowledge is based on ignorance—on an illusion (**maya**). **There is no elephant!** There is only a bunch of women.

To realize the truth, simply remove the ignorance. The appearance of the world is due to the creative illusion of maya.

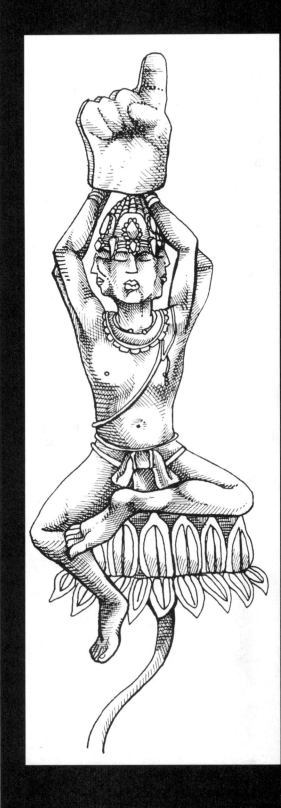

> The essence of the individual Self, the Atman, is the same as the essence of the universal Self, Brahman.
> We can realize Brahman through right knowledge or **Jnana Yoga**.

Another great teacher of Vedanta was the 11th-century saint **Ramanuja**. He was a devotee of the God Vishnu, and constructed many temples to him. He felt that no matter how evolved a person may become, there will always be his personal God whom he worships, and adores- and who will always be superior to him. Thus, there is always a duality between the self of the worshipper, and God. The self cannot be dissolved into God. Yet the many selves that worship God, and the world they live in are nothing but Brahman, or God. They have no existence apart from God. Also, the world is as real as Brahman. But Brahman can only be known through its attributes—through worship of a **personal** God. Therefore, Ramanuja teaches a **qualified non-dualism**, in which freedom arrives through devotion to a personal God.

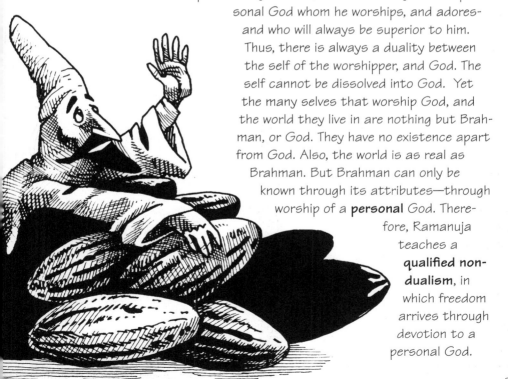

The third great teacher of Vedanta is **Madhva** (1197-1276), who taught a dualistic system. For Madhva, "difference" and "dependence" are key terms. Even in everyday life, everything depends upon something else: the husband depends upon his wife, the trees depend upon the rain. According to Madhva, matter and souls, though as real as God, depend upon Him. For Madhva, no two things are alike. Everything is different from everything else, and there are five sorts of difference:

* between God and soul
* between God and matter
* between soul and matter
* between one soul and another
* between one form of matter and another

For Madhava, the way to moksha or enlightenment is to cultivate detachment from one's actions, and a continuous feeling of devotion to God. Gradually, through studying the scriptures, one becomes aware of God's attributes, and sees God as the only independent reality. Finally, through God's grace, the devotee obtains a direct vision of God.

Alice: Well, what happened next?

Caterpillar: India was invaded, again.

In this period Muslim armies invaded much of Northern India, bringing with them a civilization carrying Arab, Jewish, Christian, Hellenistic, and Byzantine cultural influences. There could not have been a worse match than the one between the Hindu and the Islamic traditions. Hindus worshipped many Gods, and Hindu society was shaped like a pyramid, with the Brahmans on top.

The Islamic rulers believed in one God, Allah, as revealed in the Qur'an. Every Muslim is equal, and must submit to Allah. The two traditions coexisted, but not without strong hostilities and mutual suspicions. Nevertheless, Sufi Muslims and Hindus and Buddhists interacted, visited each others shrines, sometimes prayed to each others' God(s) for a good harvest, and swapped ideas in the spheres of music, dance, architecture, and painting.

The invaders found the peaceful Buddhist monasteries to be easy targets. What few Buddhists were left in India, or had not been absorbed into Hinduism, simply disappeared. In order to distinguish themselves from their Muslim overlords, the Hindus became more Hindu, becoming more fanatical in their vegetarianism, putting a greater emphasis on nonviolence, and emphasizing their worship of cows.

The Hindus also formed militant groups of naked yogis trained in the Indian martial arts. They carried tridents, and defended the monasteries from Muslim (and even Hindu) hostilities. But the major religious development during this period was the remarkable increase in devotional (bhakti) sects.

Tamil poet—saints dedicated to both Vishnu and Shiva flourished in Southern India. And a

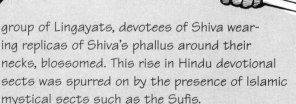

group of Lingayats, devotees of Shiva wearing replicas of Shiva's phallus around their necks, blossomed. This rise in Hindu devotional sects was spurred on by the presence of Islamic mystical sects such as the Sufis.

Kabir

In fact, the Hindu and Muslim devotional groups influenced each other. The poet **Kabir**, for instance, combines both Hindu and Islamic elements in his mystical poetry:

> **The barber has sought God,**
> **The washerwoman, and the carpenter.**
> **Even Raidas was a seeker after God.**
> **The Rishi Swapacha was a tanner by caste.**
> **Hindus and Muslims alike have achieved that End,**
> **where remains no mark of distinction.**

Kabir also transcended both the Hindu and Muslim traditions, saying that he was "neither of the temple, nor the mosque." He taught a religion of love, beyond caste distinctions.

Sikhism

Guru Nanak also combined Hindu and Muslim elements in the **Sikh** religion which he founded. Upset by the constant violence between Hindus and Muslims in India, he taught that God is infinite, and can be known through the grace of a true teacher, or guru.

Nanak also believed that the life of an ascetic did not lead to God. One should work hard, repeat the name of God, and be charitable. He felt that all were equal in the eyes of God.

Alice: So Hinduism has been changing all along, with every historical and philosophical wave that has swept over India.

Caterpillar: That's right. And Hinduism would change yet again—for once again, it was invaded.

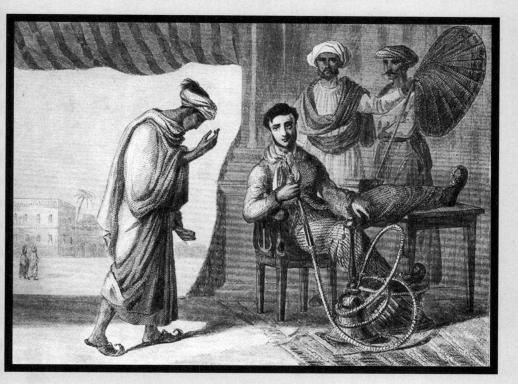

THE INDO-ANGLICAN TRUNK
(1757-PRESENT)

The British, when they conquered India, were especially appalled by the Indian treatment of women: Hindu widows entered the flames of the funeral pyre where their husbands were burning, young Indian girls were married to much older Indian men, a Hindu husband could have as many wives as he pleased, girls were often killed at birth. The British brought with them their educational system, their legal system, and the Christian religion. Though only 2.5 percent of India is today Christian, Hinduism assimilated the reform and missionary spirit of the Christian missionaries, whom they hated, adopting many of its proselytizing techniques. TWO TYPES OF HINDU RELIGIOUS GROUPS SPRANG UP IN THE PERIOD.

NEO-HINDU REFORM MOVEMENTS

The first was concerned with reforming Hindu ways: ending the caste system, calling for better treatment of women, and spreading their own brand of Hinduism using the techniques of Protestant missionaries. These movements also backed India's independence from Great Britain.

One such movement was **Rammohun Roy's *Brahmo Samaj*, or *Society of God***. Roy believed in the Vedas, but copying his Christian overlords, preached a brand of monotheistic Hinduism.

Another such organization was the **Prarthana Samaj**, or **Prayer Society of Keshub Chunder Sen**. Also copying the Christians, they formed devotional prayer groups-which were Hindu. The **Arya Samaj**, or **Aryan Society**, formed by **Swami Dayananda Sarasvati**, was a reaction to Western influences, and reasserted the Hindu Vedas as the only true path. The **Ramakrishna Mission**, founded by **Swami Vivekananda**, to this day runs schools, colleges, and hospitals in India, and has missions in the Americas and Europe.

Mahatma Gandhi, though he did not start a religious movement, worked politically for the independence of India by pursuing a strategy of nonviolent resistance to the British.

NEO-HINDU INTERNATIONAL MOVEMENTS

Timothy Leary, hippy girls reeking of sex and pachouli, John Lennon wailing "I'd **love** to turn you on," and the giggling, flower-wielding guru known as **Maharishi**—such was the summer of 1968, the Summer of Love. Most of those hippy chicks are no longer hippies, and Timothy Leary and John Lennon are dead, but the Maharishi lives on, comfortably ruling his vast international meditation empire from his Vedically designed home in Holland.

Life is Bliss!

The **Transcendental Meditation movement, which he founded in 1959**, has grown into a huge empire with millions of followers. In India alone, 65,000 school children practice the mantra-based Transcendental Meditation technique, and other followers around the world include heads of state such as Margaret Thacher and the President of Mozambique.

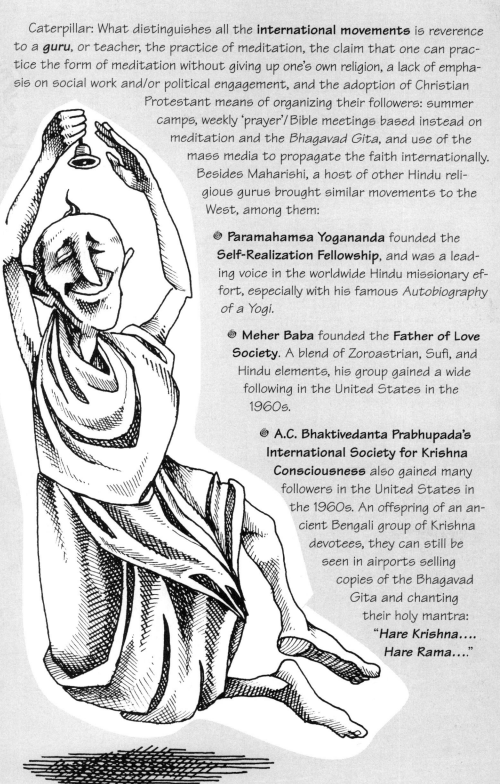

Caterpillar: What distinguishes all the **international movements** is reverence to a **guru**, or teacher, the practice of meditation, the claim that one can practice the form of meditation without giving up one's own religion, a lack of emphasis on social work and/or political engagement, and the adoption of Christian Protestant means of organizing their followers: summer camps, weekly 'prayer'/Bible meetings based instead on meditation and the Bhagavad Gita, and use of the mass media to propagate the faith internationally. Besides Maharishi, a host of other Hindu religious gurus brought similar movements to the West, among them:

◉ **Paramahamsa Yogananda** founded the **Self-Realization Fellowship**, and was a leading voice in the worldwide Hindu missionary effort, especially with his famous *Autobiography of a Yogi*.

◉ **Meher Baba** founded the **Father of Love Society**. A blend of Zoroastrian, Sufi, and Hindu elements, his group gained a wide following in the United States in the 1960s.

◉ **A.C. Bhaktivedanta Prabhupada's International Society for Krishna Consciousness** also gained many followers in the United States in the 1960s. An offspring of an ancient Bengali group of Krishna devotees, they can still be seen in airports selling copies of the Bhagavad Gita and chanting their holy mantra:
"Hare Krishna....
Hare Rama...."

- **Swami Muktananda**, founder of the **Siddha Yoga** movement also gained popularity in the United States from the 1960s through the 1970s. After his death, the move-ment was carried on, amid various controversies, mainly by his disciple, **Gurumayi Chidvilasananda**.

- **Satya Sai Baba** is another guru who has attracted a large worldwide following, though he has never left India. Reputed to be able to perform various miracles, especially healing, he has a following of 10 million worldwide.

- Strongly opposed to all these movements, and to any religion, theology, philosophy, or political system of thought was **Krishnamurti**.

> **Krishnamurti: A cup is useful only when it is empty; and a mind that is filled with beliefs, with dogmas and assertions, with quotations is really an uncreative mind; it is merely a repetitive mind.**

Alice: "A cup that is empty...." That sounds very familiar!

Caterpillar: Actually, Krishnamurti is repeating something Lao Tzu said—which gets us to our next topic.

THE PHILOSOPHIES AND RELIGIONS OF CHINA

From India, walk northeast. Traverse the Himalayas, through Tibet, until you reach the Kunlun mountains. Along their eastern slopes, you will find massed young pines standing haughtily erect. Dizzy precipices gathering blue hues. Ethereal curtains of water arc forward, sailing into the Void. Dark gorges, obscure grottoes, thunder. Swelling through distant passes, black cloud formations bruise the sky. The mountains turn cool in the darkening rain. Churning and lunging over rumbling boulders, pent-up waters drag uprooted trees. Pushing through narrow gorges, booming like cannon, they plunge between cliffs spilt by their roar. Drifting downstream, luxuriant forests of bamboo line both banks.

Your boatmen refrain from sounding the watch-drums, so as not to attract tigers. Mosquitoes are as fierce as wasps. Inside, the gorge is dark as a grotto. Cliffs rise straight up on both sides, and far overhead a narrow strip of sky shines like a ribbon of glossy blue silk. The thunder of the rapids grows louder and louder, like a violent storm of lightning and wind. The river descends onto the plains. The plains are dotted with clusters of thatched huts, bamboo fences, willows on the banks, orchards, and gardens.

Everywhere people fish with lines, pulling in nets. Along the banks little markets sell fish and crabs, cheap as dirt. Lots of little boys hawk water chestnuts, water lily seeds, lotus roots. Boats belonging to peddlers and travelers tied up bow-to-stern, form an unbroken line. Along the banks are chickens, hogs, dogs, vegetable gardens. In the evenings, the moonlight is as bright as day on the great river. Big turtles bob up and down in the water. Waves stretch to the horizon, far away. The moon's reflection moves across the water, swaying and simmering endlessly, like a golden dragon.

Ni hao, Alice! You are in China.

Alice: **Ni hao**? What kind of language is that?

Caterpillar: Chinese! Language is important in China, as in India. Whereas India's Sanskrit language is well-suited to express universal essences and abstract notions, Chinese is just the opposite. There are over a dozen ways to say "horse" or "mountain" in Chinese, but often no way to express abstract ideas and metaphysical concepts. For instance, if you want to say "contradiction" in Chinese, the expression you use is "halberd and shield."

Unlike English, written Chinese is not made up of 26 or so letters representing sounds. It is made of thousands and thousands of little paintings. If you wanted to write "tree" in ancient China, you drew a picture of it.

Thus Chinese philosophy tends to be concrete, practical, and down-to-earth: to emphasize this world rather than the next, to express the particular thing rather than the universal essence. But Chinese is also a richly suggestive and ambiguous language—lending itself to poetry. A single word, like **Jen** can mean "a man, men, some men, or mankind." So a scholar reading a philosophical text can interpret it in many ways.

The Chinese made a tradition of tradition. They revere the past, especially the distant, prehistoric past.

And the Chinese often view their philosophical history as a succession of unfolding seasons: Spring, Summer, Autumn, and Winter.

The Spring Period is shrouded in deep mystery, as only myths of sage emperors and ancient practices such as bone and turtle-shell oracles survived. Yet, it was as also in this period that "The Hundred Schools" of Chinese philosophy arose, six of which were prominent:

- The Cosmological School (also called the **Ying-Yang** School)
- The Confucian School
- The Taoists
- The School of Names
- Mo Tzu
- The Legalists

During the **Summer Flowering** (206 B.C.-900 A.D.), Buddhism bloomed in China, an exotic, alien fragrance— yet one that lent to the clear, but bland Confucian aroma, and to the dark, feminine Taoist odor, a scent both lucid and deep.

During the **Autumn Period** (960-1912), the prominence of Buddhism faded, with Neo-Confucianism attempting to recapture "authentic Chinese thought."

In the **Winter Period** (1912- ?), Western ideas such as Marxism, democracy, and postmodernism awaken the Chinese to the rest of the world.

The Spring Period

CONFUCIUS

Alice: Who was **Confucius?**
Caterpillar: Whereas most of Western philosophy is merely a footnote

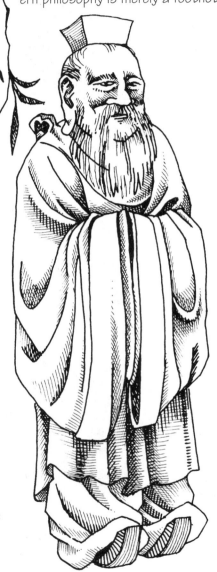

to Plato, most of Chinese philosophy and culture is merely a footnote to Confucius. Confucius is the Latinized way of saying **K'ung Fu Tzu**, or **Master Kung**. He was easy in his manner, and cheerful; gentle yet firm; dignified but not harsh; respectful, yet well at ease. When someone sang a song he liked, he would ask them to repeat it, and join in the second time.

Born in humble circumstances, he lived during one of the most turbulent times in Chinese history. All under Heaven was in chaos. The code of chivalrous honor had degenerated into sheer horror. China's feudal states were perpetually at war. And war was not only more frequent but more severe. Entire populations of hundreds of thousands were beheaded, including women, children, and the aged. Or they were thrown into boiling cauldrons and their loved ones were forced to drink the human soup.

It was called the **Period of the Hundred Philosophers**, for all the warfare stimulated much concern. Wandering scholars proliferated, each with his own solution to the horrors of the times. Feudal lords began searching out and accepting the advice of all manner of freelance philosophers (Confucius was one of these), strategists, pacifists, moralists, soldiers of fortune, and charlatans.

If a strategist's advice failed, he would often be summarily sawn in half, pulled limb from limb by horses, or boiled. In this climate of undiluted bloodshed, the ideas of Confucius were considered revolutionary—and impractical. Luckily for him, nobody asked his advice.

Alice: Well, what were his ideas?

Caterpillar: The most important thing for Confucius was **Jen**, or human kindness, love of man. Jen is the ideal feeling of warmth, kindness, dignity, and respect that should develop between two people. It is not the love of God, but the natural human love one feels for one's parents, brothers, and superiors.

Alice: But how does one cultivate Jen?

Caterpillar: Confucius, whom the Chinese call "The First Teacher," felt that Jen could be cultivated by **Li**, or the practice of social norms such as rites, rituals, ceremonies, good manners, courtesy, and etiquette. In the words of Confucius, "In order to establish oneself, one has to establish others." Through practicing good moral behavior, morality becomes habitual, and a person gains Jen. All of this depends upon education, for by studying the standards of moral behavior and virtue and proper relationship in the **Confucian Classics**, one can become a realized human being.

Alice: Proper relationship?

Caterpillar: Confucius believed in "the rectification of names," so that people should be as they are named. The ruler should be a ruler, the subject should be a subject, the father a father, the son a son.

Alice: Well, what about the **Classics?**

Caterpillar: Traditionally, the **Confucian Classics** form a body of literature supposedly about the ancient beginnings of Chinese society. Study of the Confucian Classics was the way to educate a man's mind and refine his character—and all through imitation of the ways of the ancestors of the ancient **Shang Dynasty.**

GEE, I FEEL BETTER ALREADY.

The **First Confucian Classic** is the *I Ching*, or the *Classic Book of Changes*. It is an oracle or book of divination that imitates in book form the ancient Shang method of divination by tortoise shells. It forms the basis of the **Cosmological School** or **Ying-yang School**. The book consists of 64 hexagrams representing the mysterious structure of the universe, and the way it changes:

> "Keeping Still, Mountain.
> Keeping his back still
> So that he no longer feels his body.
> He goes into his courtyard
> And does not see his people.
> No blame."

The **Second Confucian Classic** is the *Shu Ching* or *Book of History*, a book of speeches, reports, and announcements of the sage-kings during the ancient dynasties. It served as a model for all Chinese rulers:

"In antiquity, Emperor Yao was reverent, intelligent, sincere, and mild."

The **Third Confucian Classic** is the *Shih Ching*, or *Book of Odes*—a book of poetry and folksongs. Politically, it is important, because it shows that when the ruler is just, the people compose odes. When the ruler is unjust, they compose satire:

> **"The doings of Heaven are soundless, and odorless.**
> **Big rat, big rat, do not eat my millet."**

The **Fourth Confucian Classic** is the *Ritual*, a collection of philosophy and rules for everyday living-etiquette.

The **Fifth Confucian Classic** is the *Ch'un-ch'iu* or *Spring and Autumn Annals*, a history of the state of Lu, probably written by Confucius in order to teach moral behavior.

The **Sixth Confucian Classic** is the Music, which was presumably a text on music, although we do not know for sure.

The *Confucian Classics* describe a moral world, but it is also a religious world, ruled on high by the God **Shang Ti** and lesser Gods such as the moon and stars, the sun, wind, rain, mountains, and rivers. Also in Heaven dwell the ancestors, to whom their heirs sacrifice in order to gain their blessings. In fact, Heaven itself is like Shang Ti, an intelligent power, guiding the destinies of men. And the **Will of Heaven** was very important to the ancients, and thus to Confucius.

But the Will of Heaven was especially important to the ruler. For, how could he perform his duties if he did not follow the Will of Heaven? This was a major issue for Chinese thinkers. The ruler was expected to set a moral example, then all of the country would follow him, like grass bending down in the wind. Confucius felt that victory would surely go to the state that achieved the highest degree of culture, the most illumined arts, the most exalted philosophy, the most sublime poetry and music.

The good ruler is therefore not one who seeks to change the way men act through laws and force. The good ruler acts morally so that others will become aware of their true nature. As Confucius writes in The Analects, "A ruler who governs by virtue can be compared to the North Star which remains fixed in its place while the other stars pay it homage."

If a ruler conducts himself uprightly, he receives the Will of Heaven, confirms his stellar position in society, and harmonizes the entire world. His conduct inspires others, who are inspired to act virtuously themselves. For centuries the Chinese have felt that if the ruler acts in accordance with Heaven, then harmony will reign in his realm.

It is true that China assimilated wave after wave of barbarian invasions through the grandeur and nobility of her culture. Many a barbarian succumbed to the spell of Chinese civilization, so much so that he forgot about plundering and raping. He only hoped to someday be mistaken for a true Confucian gentleman, with his chief desire to write an essay on the **Classics**, or a poem his Chinese tutor would find worthy.

Herein lies the great Confucian triumph and the pacifist reputation of the Chinese. Confucius believed that waves of virtuous influence radiated from the moral nucleus of the Emperor, passing through the immediate environment within China, and extending even to the populations and rulers of surrounding non-Chinese barbarian states.

This may have not been the case for all leaders, but it was certainly the case for Confucius.

CAN I COME IN? I PROMISE TO BE GOOD...

Two hundred years after his death, his philosophy became the official state philosophy. And to this day his thought still exerts its influence in China, Singapore, Taiwan, and even Japan, which bow down to it like grasses in the wind.

MENCIUS

Caterpillar: If Confucius was the Socrates of China, **Mencius** (**Meng Tzu,** 372-289 B.C.), was China's Plato—the man who made Confucius known to all. He once stated that he wanted to become "a second Confucius," and indeed, since his death, he has been known as "The Second Sage." Mencius was born about a century after Confucius. After studying with **Tzu Ssu,** a disciple of Confucius's grandsons, he traveled from ruler to ruler, preaching virtue. The rulers, however, were more interested in warfare than Confucian morality, so, like Confucius, Mencius settled down to a life of teaching and writing. Whereas Confucius taught that people who behave morally could strive to become gentlemen, Mencius was more optimistic. He felt sure that anyone could become a sage-king!

Alice: Wow! How can I do that?

Well, you couldn't because you are a woman. In ancient China, poor families often left their daughters to die of exposure in the fields. If the girl should survive this attempted infanticide, her principal function was to marry and to bear children—preferably sons. Secondarily, she was a housekeeper.

> Her only other options were to be sold into slavery or prostitution. Without education, if she married, she was subjected to the tyranny of her mother-in-law. She was forced to stay at home while her husband dallied with his young mistresses and concubines, and she was permanently subservient.

However, according to Mencius, everyone, from the very beginning, is good. Heaven or **T'ien** endows everyone with four virtues at birth:

- ◇ **Jen**, human kindness
- ◇ **I**, righteousness
- ◇ **Li**, courteousness
- ◇ **Chih**, wisdom.

These are innate in human nature. If they are cultivated, then men can become sage-kings.

Alice: Innate?

Caterpillar: Yes, for instance, if we see a child about to fall into a deep well, our heart goes out to the child. We attempt to rescue it. It is just as natural for us to do good as it is for water to flow downwards.

For Mencius, "oughtness," or righteousness, was just as important as Jen (human kindness). One should resort to "oughtness" in every situation with every person. I, or "oughtness," is a sense of the proper thing to do in every situation—even if it means sacrificing one's own life.

If it was important for the average citizen to behave properly, it was mandatory for the ruler. In ruling the empire, the ruler should appeal to innate human virtues of the masses. This will capture their hearts. If he rules in this way, he rules under the Will of Heaven. The Will of Heaven is like an imperial driver's license issued from Heaven. There is only one catch—it could be taken away if the ruler didn't act properly.

The ruler, after all, exists not for himself, but for the sake of the governed. If he gives them peace and plenty, educates them to develop their innate virtue, and performs rites to the forces of nature so that nature stays on the side of the farmer, he rules with the Will of Heaven.

But if he oppresses the people or attempts to rule by force, or is so unfortunate as to rule during a drought, flood, or plague, then he is no longer following the Will of Heaven. He loses his imperial driver's license. The people then have the right to revolt. For he ceases being a ruler and becomes "a robber and ruffian we call a mere fellow," and such a "mere fellow" is often put to death.

As Mencius said, if such a "mere fellow were put to death, I have never heard that is assassinating a ruler." In actual fact, Chinese emperors praised Mencius, but seldom were they able to live up to his teachings.

Mencius also developed a theory of land distribution, which has never actually been put into practice. His plan called for dividing a square mile of land so that it resembles the Chinese character for "well," **ching**. The inner square is public land, and the remaining eight squares belong each to one of eight families. They all contribute to the cultivation of the central plot, with the profit from the harvests going to the ruler.

Confucius and Mencius taught that man was good, and this inner goodness could be developed through proper education. One's innate compassion could be developed into human kindness, one's innate sense of shame could be developed into "oughtness," etc.

Alice: But are humans innately good?

Caterpillar: That's the assumption that Hsun Tzu challanged.

HSUN TZU

Hsun Tzu (300-215 B.C.), considered one of the great Confucians, was not so optimistic, and disagreed on a fundamental point. He states flatly, "The nature of man is evil; his goodness is only acquired through artifice or training." A hard-headed realist, he observed that men's emotions and desires are more often selfish than benign. Men don't just feel compassion and human kindness; they also experience love, hate, anger, grief. These instinctive emotions, if developed, would lead to violent crimes and suffering.

Hsun Tzu is Confucian to the core in his belief that animalistic human nature can be whipped into shape by education, the example of the leadership of the sages, rites, and music.

SQUARE ? I AIN'T NOTHIN' BUT HEP.

Regarding funeral rites, he was unconcerned with their effect on the dead. He was humanistic, more concerned with their ability to express the emotions of the living. He felt that music could perfect and express human emotions as well. He saw the social realm, the realm of Heaven, and the realm of earth as entirely separate. Thus, earthquakes are not due to the immoral actions of any ruler. His view that Heaven helps those who help themselves and that religion is more effective in shaping human morals than in influencing divine beings remained the Confucian teaching throughout Chinese history.

Any system of thought, however, is closed, and cannot begin to contain the overflowing complexity of life in its entirety. The Confucian system was no exception. Confucius, for all the positive influence he exercised, was something of a square. Deeply concerned with order and the creation of social harmony, he refused to sit on his mat if it was not laid out symmetrically, and ate no meat unless it was cut out in perfect little cubes. He taught that the natural flow of human behavior should be channeled by education and numerous rules and laws. The morality, poise, dignity, and courtesy preached by Confucius may have thwarted aggression; but it also repressed individualism, emotion, spontaneity, pleasure, curiosity, creativity, the spirit of adventure, and experience of mystical transcendence.

Alice: Then how did the Chinese let their hair down?

TAOISM

Caterpillar: Almost by necessity, Chinese Confucian culture bore within itself an alter ego, a tendency to differ from and violate itself, to transgress its own system of values, to unravel and reconstruct itself into its shadowy opposite. The rule-bound traditionalism carried within itself the trace of its opposite, tending to produce the very values it forbade.

Alice: This sounds mysterious!

Caterpillar: Yes, it is mysterious. But perhaps we can understand it better if we approach it artistically. Imagine a Chinese landscape painting.

We are first struck by a sense of sheer vastness.
In the upper right corner juts an eccentric, jagged peak.
Diagonally opposite a river twists and turns, like
the tail of a dragon. Most of the canvas, however, is
a sea of bright mist. Billowing nothingness.
Shining void.

Occasionally, barely visible among these luminous vacuities, towering precipices, waterfalls, rocky crags, and tortured pines, we may find a minuscule human figure. This is the **Taoist** hermit. Crossing a rustic bridge, or sitting atop a rock, he languishes, plucking his lute, leaning against his bamboo staff, drinking in the view, or secluded in a hut of bamboo, meditating on the moon, painting a poem or a landscape on a scroll of rice paper, serenely aloof from the mundane affairs of worldly men.

Alice: Taoist hermit? What is the *Tao*?

Caterpillar: According to the Tao's most talkative missionaries, it cannot be talked about. Any attempt to describe it is something like using a bear trap to capture a butterfly or a mud dike to abate the Hwang Ho River. "Hazy and indistinct it is," they tell us, "vague and mysterious."

The **Taoist Classics** comprise some 122 chapters. **Lao Tzu**, Taoism's legendary founder, jotted down 81 terse and enigmatic poems. **Chuang Tzu**, or rather his disciples, recorded 33 chapters brimming with fantasy, lyricism, and nonsense. And **Leih Tzu** wrote eight, which were long-winded, poetic, and vague.

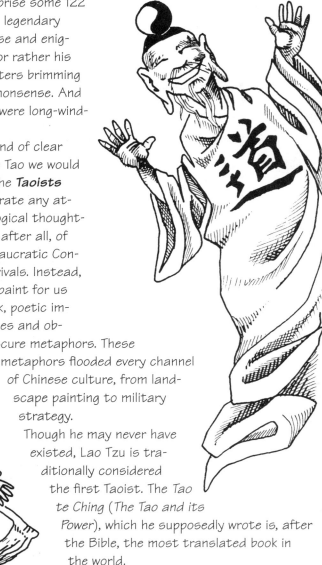

Nowhere do we find the kind of clear categorical definition of the Tao we would expect of a Western text. The **Taoists Classics** intentionally frustrate any attempt at categorical and logical thought—the language, after all, of their bureaucratic Confucian rivals. Instead, they paint for us dark, poetic images and obscure metaphors. These metaphors flooded every channel of Chinese culture, from landscape painting to military strategy.

Though he may never have existed, Lao Tzu is traditionally considered the first Taoist. The *Tao te Ching* (*The Tao and its Power*), which he supposedly wrote is, after the Bible, the most translated book in the world.

TZU WHO?

Taoists conceive of a universe composed of **Yin** and **Yang**. Yin and Yang are in continual flux, giving rise to light and dark, male and female, heat and cold, hardness and softness. The Yang light of noon always contains a trace of its opposite, the Yin darkness of midnight. Yin and Yang are ceaselessly ebbing and flowing back and forth in an endless play of differences, just like Confucianism and Taoism.

Standing beyond the play of Yin and Yang is the spiritual essence the universe—Tao. Nevertheless, Lao Tzu characterizes the Tao in ns of the feminine, the Yin. For instance, he speaks of the supple ength of beings and things normally consid- soft and weak, such as nen, babies, and water: "Tao he softest thing in the ld, but it can over- ne the hardest ng in the world." Water has no con- stant form and over- comes the hard and strong be- cause of its erosive softness, endurance, plia- bility, shameless- ness, and nonrigidity. The Tao is the Primordial Female, the Mystical Womb, the Mother of the 10,000 Creatures. All things continually emerge from her dark feminine fecundity.

The Mystical Womb of the Tao is empty. Just as the dark vacuity of space spawns galaxies, the emptiness of the womb generates a living child, and a teacup holds tea precisely where it isn't. The Tao cradles and nurtures all things by virtue of its emptiness. The hub of the wheel, the empty space in the pot, the nothingness in the door and window give the spokes, the pot, and the room their utility. Intangible is the Tao—elusive, obscure, evasive, inaudible, formless, imageless, shadowy, and perplexing, too subtle to be perceived by the senses.

Alice: Were there other famous Taoists?
Caterpillar: The most important, besides Lao Tzu, was Chuang Tzu.

Chuang Tzu

Caterpillar: One of the major themes in Taoist literature is that of the Confucian emperor seeking out the Taoist sage deeply hidden in his cloud-wrapped mountain hermitage. Dating from the 4th century B.C., the **Chuang Tzu**, written by a hermit of that name, provides an early example:

Once, when Chuang Tzu was fishing in the P'u River, the kind Ch'u sent two officials to go and announce to him: "I would like to trouble you with the administration of my realm."

Chuang Tzu: I have heard that there is a sacred tortoise in Ch'u that has been dead for 3,000 years. The king keeps it wrapped in cloth and boxed, and stores it in the ancestral temple. Now would this tortoise rather be dead and have its bones left behind and honored? Or would it rather be alive and dragging its tail in the mud?

The Two Officials: It would rather be alive and dragging its tail in the mud.

Chuang Tzu: Go away! I'll drag my tail in the mud!

Caterpillar: So sought after were Taoist hermits that many impostors became hermits, just so that they might get a political position. In the T'ang Dynasty, this practice was so widespread that a popular proverb surfaced: "Retiring to the mountains is a short cut." Embracing quietude, reclusion, exile, and the rejection of public service, became the best way to get a civil service job—without even having to pass the examinations.

Alice: Is Taoism good for anything else, other than wagging your tail in the mud—and getting a government job?

Caterpillar: Confucius never talked about extraordinary things: like Gods, war, and sex. For these we have to turn to Taoism.

Military Strategy

The **Warring States Period** began just a quarter of a century after the death of Confucius, rather rudely. The leaders of three small states attacked the leader of another, defeated him, divided his domain among themselves, cut off the head of its ruler, killed his family, and used his skull for a drinking cup. The fighting and marching never stopped. Horses of slain soldiers neighed piteously into the empty air. Crops were destroyed, and only decaying bodies and white bones lay in the fields. Crows and hawks pecked at the open wounds for human guts, carried them in their beaks, and hung them from the branches of withered trees.

109

One of the many wandering strategists looking for a job during the Warring States Period, was **Sun Tzu**. He wrote a book called *The Art of War*, which has a definite Taoist influence. Instead of the direct lines of force, square, angular formations, and massive frontal attacks favored in Western warfare, Sun Tzu amassed infinitely fluid formations, drawing in the enemy like a woman draws in a man, by appearing to yield, then liquefying, dispersing, spiraling around him like a whirlpool, and after a dizzying mirage of evolutions, surrounding, crushing, and sucking his essence with a sudden concentration of force.

Sun Tzu's perfect army avoids the enemy's strengths, withdrawing like lightning and leaving only a void.

The perfect army is aqueous, like water, fluid formations as inexhaustible as the flow of great rivers, or those of a passionate woman.

Bedroom Arts : Clouds and Rain (Taoist Sexual Techniques)
A branch of plum blossoms is silhouetted against a full moon. Reflected in the dark lake, the galaxy spews light like a dizzy cloud of fireflies. Far in the distance, horses and carriages pass almost silently. Amid the whispering fragrance of pines, a pleasure pavilion gathers the moonlight like white jade. The night deepens. A light mist rises off the lake and mixes with the pine fragrance. Mountain birds cry plaintively in the distance. Now and again, moans sound softly from the pavilion. A gentle breeze penetrates the curtains and drifts through the room past a pair of white egrets, fluttering eternally on a painted screen.

Behind, a young woman's body tenses. The golden pin falls from her hair, her eyes disappear under their lids, her nostrils widen, and her face flushes. Her lover's "jade stalk" drifts dreamily, advancing and retreating within her "solitary valley," like a fish weaving upstream against the current. A Taoist emperor is blending **Yin** and **Yang** with one of his twelve hundred concubines. She opens her lips and her teeth shine. Her tongue stiffens and swells. A warm scent rises from the pillows. Her **Yin** tide is flooding.

It is written that the emperor never ejaculated, never slept, and had the vigor of 10 young men. By means of the energy derived from the art of the bedchamber, he attained an immortal body and ascended to Heaven in broad daylight. In Heaven, he continued his amorous ways, this time with celestial damsels.

The most ancient manuals describing Taoist sexual techniques have come down from the **Han period** (206 B.C.-220 A.D). Despite puritanical Confucian and ascetic Buddhist efforts to repress them, Taoism stubbornly persisted in Chinese bedrooms. The practices themselves were a blend of secular necessity and sacred wisdom.

By the Han period, matriarchal society had disappeared, and Chinese households were polygamous. The earliest sexual teachings seem to have been concerned only with the prolongation of sexual pleasure, and ensuring that the female was satisfied before the male. That way, male and female emissions would intermingle and the harmony of Yin and Yang, clouds and rain, would be achieved. As monogamy gave way to polygamy, however, almost any man of means maintained several wives as well as a number of maidservants and concubines.

If a man tried to satisfy the sexual needs of all the women in his household by conventional methods, he would soon collapse from exhaustion. On the other hand, if he failed to satisfy the women, his household would not be harmonious—and this, too, could have dire consequences.

Yet, since women are nearly inexhaustible sources of vital energy, a wise husband should be able to fill himself to overflowing with energy rather than expend himself carelessly.

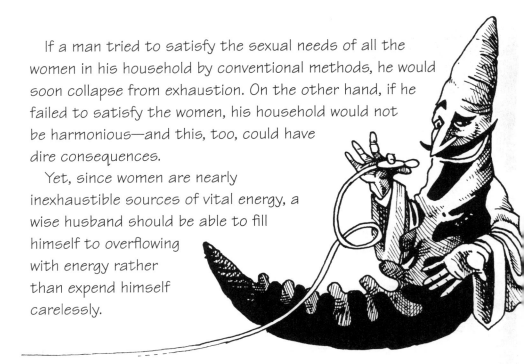

What he needed was the Taoist approach.

For the Taoists, sexual intercourse and erotic play were powerful means of stimulating and amplifying the Yin in women and the Yang in men. Through orgasm, however, this accumulation of vital force is thrown off in the form of sexual fluids, which can then be absorbed by one's sexual partner. Thus, if a man can absorb the Yin juices of his lover's vagina while refraining from ejaculation, he wins her vital force and augments his own.

The Taoist arts of the bedchamber advise men how to control their own sexual nature, how to give pleasure to their partners, and how to accumulate and circulate vital energy. By varying the speed, angle, and general feel of his movements, the good Taoist lover could bring forth his lovers Yin tide. Bucking like a wild horse through a mountain stream, or plunging very deeply, like a huge stone sinking into the sea or veering from side to side, like the long slow swerves made by a larg carp when caught on the hook, he sipped and licked up the juices of his lover's "three peaks": her mouth, her breasts, and her vagina.

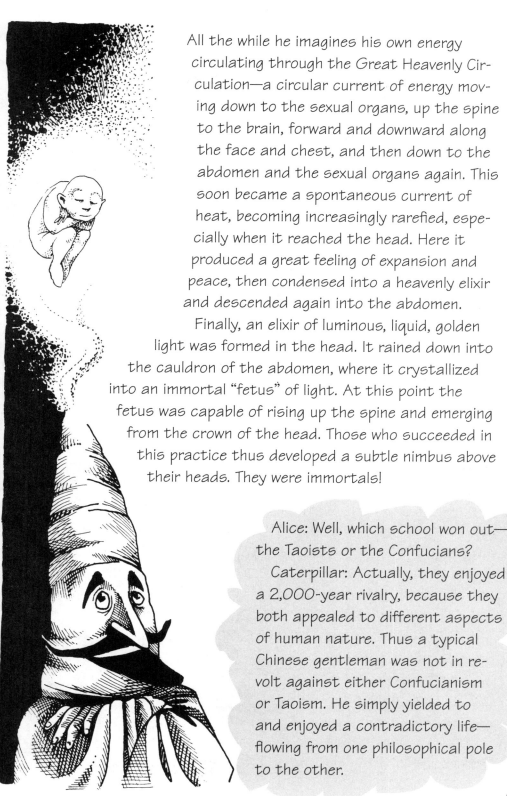

All the while he imagines his own energy circulating through the Great Heavenly Circulation—a circular current of energy moving down to the sexual organs, up the spine to the brain, forward and downward along the face and chest, and then down to the abdomen and the sexual organs again. This soon became a spontaneous current of heat, becoming increasingly rarefied, especially when it reached the head. Here it produced a great feeling of expansion and peace, then condensed into a heavenly elixir and descended again into the abdomen.

Finally, an elixir of luminous, liquid, golden light was formed in the head. It rained down into the cauldron of the abdomen, where it crystallized into an immortal "fetus" of light. At this point the fetus was capable of rising up the spine and emerging from the crown of the head. Those who succeeded in this practice thus developed a subtle nimbus above their heads. They were immortals!

Alice: Well, which school won out—the Taoists or the Confucians?

Caterpillar: Actually, they enjoyed a 2,000-year rivalry, because they both appealed to different aspects of human nature. Thus a typical Chinese gentleman was not in revolt against either Confucianism or Taoism. He simply yielded to and enjoyed a contradictory life—flowing from one philosophical pole to the other.

A Chinese male could be strictly orthodox in all his Confucian family roles—meek toward his father, respectful to his uncles, a strict disciplinarian to his wife, sternly advising to his younger brothers, ruinously indulgent towards his small son—and totally moonstruck with his 15-year-old concubine.

In his hours with her, he would abandon all Confucian decorum, and apply the Taoist arts of "clouds and rain." Then, all day long at the office, he would dream of becoming a Taoist hermit, deep within the pine mountains.

One Taoist story sums up the often humorous rivalry between Confucianism and Taoism for the Chinese spirit. It concerns a Taoist hermit who was sitting alone in his bamboo hut, meditating.

Suddenly he was disturbed by a group of Confucian do-gooders who had scaled the mountain to give him a lecture on virtue and morality.

When they set foot inside his hut, they exclaimed: "What are you doing sitting naked in your hut—meditating? You should put on your pants."

The hermit responded, "The entire universe is my hut. This little bamboo hut is just my pants. What are you fellows doing inside my pants?"

THE SCHOOL OF NAMES

Kung Sun Lung (320-250 B.C.) is famous for his paradox,

"A white horse is not a horse!"

Alice: What?

Caterpillar: According to legend, a border guard stopped Kung Sun Lung, who was riding a white horse. The border guard informed him that horses were not allowed across the border.

Kung Sun Lung: But I am riding a white horse, and a white horse is not a horse!

Guard: What?

Kung Sun Lung: Suppose you ask me for a horse.

Guard: Okay.

Kung Sun Lung: If I bring you a yellow horse or a black horse, then you will be happy—right?

Guard: Right.

Kung Sun Lung: But suppose you ask me for a white horse.

Guard: Okay.

Kung Sun Lung: If I bring you a yellow or black horse, you will not be happy, right?

Guard: Right.

Kung Sun Lung: Therefore, a white horse is not a horse!

MO TZU

Mo Tzu (470-381 B.C.), was born shortly after the death of Confucius, and died just before Mencius was born. During that time, he founded the school of **Mohism**, that became the chief rival of Confucianism.

The Mohists were an austere group, clothed in coarse cloth and sandals, and willing to walk for days to go the assistance of those who needed their help. For many years, Mo Tzu was a roaming political philosopher. He taught that Heaven, **T'ien**, was a personal and benevolent presence that showered down universal love on all men. Men can follow the example of Heaven by giving up partiality.

Alice: Partiality?

Partiality, or particularity, is selfishness: seeking gain only for one's immediate family or state. Such partiality destroys society. You are only nice to certain people in particular. According to Mo Tzu, one should attempt to overcome partiality by extending universal love and benevolence to all, just as Heaven does. Mo Tzu was especially against warfare. He and his followers would journey long distances to attempt to pacify a ruler about to invade a defenseless state. Should they fail in their peace-keeping mission, they would often go to the aid of the invaded state. For this reason, Mo Tzu wrote on the defensive aspects of military strategy. Mohists abandoned all activities which did not directly contribute to providing food, shelter, and clothing for everyone. For this reason, they attacked many Confucian values:

- Listening to loud music, for instance, was an important part of the Confucian ethic. Mo Tzu felt that one should abandon listening to music.

- Confucius praised the value of rituals, especially funerals, but Mo Tzu felt that elaborate funerals were a waste of time and money, and that long periods of mourning that forbade sexual intercourse were a menace to society.

- Mo Tzu was more religious than Confucius, and condemned his agnosticism and neglect of spirits and spiritual values.

- Mo Tzu also felt that Confucius was fatalistic.

After Mo Tzu's death, Mohism posed a major philosophical threat to Confucianism. Mencius attacked the Mohist ideal of universal benevolence. According to Confucius, one's feelings of human kindness are always expressed within the circle of one's own special interests and loyalties. Human kindness is measured out differently to a ruler, a father, a daughter. If everyone loved everyone universally, the entire Confucian system of the five relationships would collapse.

Instead, Mo Tzu's popularity collapsed. After all, his way was too austere for most Chinese. His school was constantly under relentless attack by Mencius. And Confucianism was adopted as the official state philosophy during the **Han Dynasty** (206 B.C.-220 A.D.).

Mo Tzu and Mohism were, thereafter, largely forgotten until Western scholars rediscovered him, and found similarities between his teaching and those of Jesus. He was also rediscovered by China's Communist revolutionaries who liked his Marxist-like ideas of supplying goods for the whole of society.

Alice: Well, Mo Tzu seems like a nice guy.

Caterpillar: Yes, but a more realistic group of philosophers made a deeper impression on Chinese thought.

THE LEGALISTS

> "Punish light crime severely."
> —Lord Shang

Caterpillar: Broil a criminal until he is charred to a black corpse, cut his heart open, pickle him, bind him with chains, sell him into slavery, cut off his limbs, make mincemeat of his intestines, throw him in a trap among brambles, toss his corpse into the Yangtze River, stone him to death, break his ribs, boil him in oil. Such were the punishments prescribed by **Legalists**—not only for common working men, but for graceful ladies, beloved concubines, feminine courtiers, lords, and ministers, should they offend the ruler. And a "criminal" didn't have to kill a ruler to receive such punishment. The penalty for dumping ashes or garbage on the streets was amputation of hands and feet.

Legalist logic: If there are no small crimes, then there will be no big crimes. Forget about cultivating the people's virtue! Punish them severely, swiftly, strictly, and uniformly—only then will they behave!

Like Hsun Tzu, the Legalists were practicing politicians enmeshed in the real world. They tended to look down on intellectuals and philosophers, especially Confucians. According to the Legalists, performing rites and learning the **Classics** will not make a person behave. Only laws will make people step into line.

Since man is innately bad, they believed that external force needed to be applied in the form of laws and order, and generous rewards and severe punishments. They believed in collective responsibility for the behavior of the individual, and in the duty of the people to produce military strength for the authoritarian state.

Under the Legalist system, the ruler didn't have to be a virtuous Confucian model of moral perfection. He could be a slick, shadowy, double-talking fraud, as long as he had put in place a legal machinery that administrators could run. These administrators thought of the state as an efficient bureaucratic machine geared for warfare to be fought by farmers prepared to drop their plough handles at a moment's notice, and to march into battle.

This attitude did increase the efficient functioning and military power of the state. The state of Ch'in, the most Legalist of all the Legalist states, rose to power, conquering its bordering states, and emerging as the First Empire.

One of the first steps the First Legalist Emperor undertook was to pickle, boil, and cut to pieces all the Confucian scholars he could round up, and burn all the Confucian books he could find. His subjects toiled like disciplined, submissive ants in the huge machinery of the legalist state. Their only purpose was to fight and produce crops. All human and moral concerns were subordinated to the greedy goals of the state.

But those who live by the sword die by the sword. Lord Shang, the Legalist philosopher whose organizing genius made the rise of the Ch'in Empire to supremacy possible, was finally slain, his head, arms, and legs ripped apart by chariots charging off in different directions.

Han Fei Tzu

Caterpillar: **Han Fei Tzu** (280-233 B.C.) was the most famous of the Legalists. He studied under Hsun Tzu, and shared his pessimism concerning the innate goodness of human nature. In the manner of all good Legalists, he felt that the selfish, self-interested ways of the people could only be mended through generous rewards and severe punishments. For Han Fei Tzu, the Confucian ideas of cultivating peoples' supposedly innate virtues through education and the moral example of the ruler were mere fantasy. He criticized the Confucian notion of romanticizing the past Golden Age of morality. He argued that in the past, people were not more virtuous. For human nature never changes. However, in the past there were fewer people, and more abundant resources. Therefore, people in the past "Golden Age" could afford to be more generous.

Han Fei Tzu, like most Legalists, believed in harsh punishment for crimes. And the government can find out who is a criminal, if they offer everyone a reward for reporting crimes. Another "Big Brother is Watching" practice he liked was punishing all the inhabitants of a village for the crimes committed by just one man in the village. This technique insured that neighbors would spy on neighbors— thereby extending the arm of the law- without the need of further police.

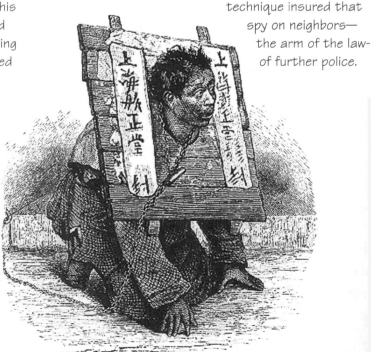

BUDDHISM IN CHINA

Caterpillar: Buddhism arrived first in the form of religious art-icons of serene, hallowed Buddhas sitting in the Lotus pose—carried by camels and yaks through the trade routes of Tibet and Central Asia and the Silk Road. To the Chinese this Buddha figure looked at first something like a Taoist Immortal.

They tended to make a god out of Buddha, sitting his image on their family altars beside their other gods, Confucius, and Lao Tzu.

> GO EAST, YOUNG YAK.

Problems only began when Buddhist ideas started to pour into China. The Chinese had always been this-worldly, practical, and down-to-earth. Nothing could have seemed more alien to them than the strange new doctrine of Buddhism, with its pessimistic First Noble Truth that life is a bummer. This floored them. And to make matters worse, Buddhism also proclaimed that release from the sorrows of the world can be achieved by the annihilation of desire(s), and ultimately blowing out the flame of the candle of existence through achieving **Nirvana**! These anti-Confucian heresies outraged the Chinese. After all, if Buddhism is so great, they argued, then why didn't Confucius tell them about it? The **Confucian Classics** don't say a thing about Buddhism!

And why do Buddhist monks do injury to their bodies by shaving their heads? Furthermore, why do they practice celibacy? If they don't have any children, then who will worship the ancestors? No Chinese should be without a child!

Why should we allow ourselves to be influenced by Indian ways? Why do monks give up worldly pleasures, such as feasting on Kung Pao Chicken and rice wine, kissing the peach-like faces of beautiful women, and undoing their hairpins? If everyone puts on Buddhist robes, these women will remain sleepless, not with love, but with loneliness, their white silk pillows growing cold in the long night.

But if the Chinese at first distrusted Buddhist thought, after a while they became fascinated, and then later, captivated. Eventually they accepted Buddhism as one of their three great philosophies, along with Confucianism and Taoism—at least for awhile.

Just as India had done, China sprouted several schools of Buddhism, each one claiming (falsely) to offer the true, original teaching of the Buddha. Of course these schools benefited greatly if they were lucky enough to receive the official support of an emperor—or an empress.

Alice: I didn't know that China ever had an empress!
Caterpillar: Only one. Empress Wu.

The Flower Garland (Hua-Yen) School

Caterpillar: On warm, fragrant moonlight evenings, she waited at the Forbidden Gate, her dark eyes searching the moonshadows. Upon hearing his horse approach in the distance, she plucked her jade hairpin, shook her hair over her shoulders, and puffed out the candle.

Often the lovers of Empress Wu were Buddhist monks. For even if its airy doctrines were somewhat beyond her considerable mental capacities, the Empress loved Buddhism.

At the age of 13, she had arrived at the Imperial Palace, the youngest and loveliest of the concubines. Wandering the imperial gardens, the carriages drifting by like flowing water, the horses like dragons, she learned how to place crimson combs in her hair, to play the lute, and to paint her face with makeup. Her silken gown rustled when she danced, and the embroidered golden phoenixes and silver geese seemed to spread their wings. Descending the golden stairs, her skirt came loose.

Could it be an omen that it is time for her to see her lord? After all, she has boasted that she can straddle and ride any horse in the empire.

Her lord, the Emperor, has invited her for a sail on the lotus lake. Untying her gauze dress, not waiting to be coaxed, but upon the pillows, waiting to be led, she is sweetly unashamed. As little wavelets pound upon the boat prow, she moans for the first time in love, while all around her, blossoming water lilies slowly yield their fragrance to the sun.

With her bewitching eyebrows, she soon became the Emperor's favorite and most cunning concubine, scheming how to seize the office of Empress! When the Emperor died, however, she was forced to join a Buddhist nunnery, where she would have passed her years withering into silence. But a new Emperor was in power, and his Empress wanted to use the beautiful Buddhist nun Wu to woo her husband away from the embraces of a concubine with whom he was enchanted.

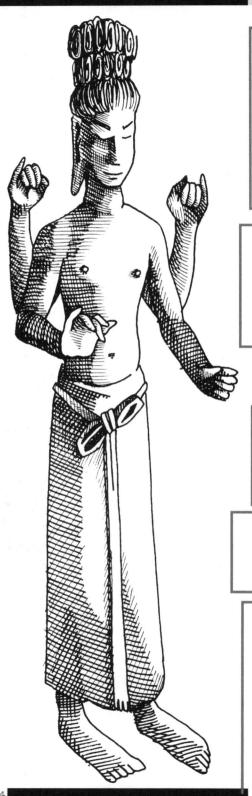

Wu, however, was not interested in acting as the pawn in anyone else's game. She succeeded in having the Empress sent away, saying that she had killed a child. Through this ruse Wu became the new Empress. When her husband died of a stroke, she swiftly killed many of her opponents, conquering the imperial throne like a silkworm devouring a mulberry leaf.

Eventually she became one of China's most able rulers ever: The Heavenly Empress. In fact, she was the only woman in all of Chinese history to become emperor. She established Buddhism as the official state religion, much to the dismay of the Taoists and Confucianists. After all, the Confucian books declared that a woman could never rule!

According to Confucius, having a woman rule would be as unnatural as hearing a hen crow like a rooster at daybreak. Empress Wu therefore set about wooing Buddhist monks instead of Confucian scholars and Taoist monks.

One Buddhist monk, a lover of the Empress, proclaimed her the earthly incarnation of **Maitreya Buddha**, as well as the World Ruler prophesied in a Buddhist scripture!

Another of the most illustrious Buddhist monks was **Fa Tsang**. He had always shown a flair for the dramatic, at the age of 16 having burned off one of his fingers and offered it to a statue of the Buddha. And when he first preached Buddhism to the Heavenly Empress, the earth shook for an entire hour. Wishing to capture the attention of Empress Wu, he dreamed up the most vivid and famous of all Buddhist images: **Indra's Net**.

lice: Isn't **Indra** a Hindu God?

Caterpillar: Yes, and Fa Tsang created a Buddhist image that is very un-Buddhist.

Alice: Un-Buddhist?

Yes. Remember that Indian philosophy is an attempt to relate the things of this world to some undying metaphysical essence, some **Great Beyond***, to relate individual existence to* **permanent cosmic existence***, to relate the many to the* **One***. Buddhism, on the other hand, abandons that kind of thinking, seeking instead to relate individual things to other individual things. Then it even calls into question their "thingness," their self-existence.*

And in fact Fa Tsang's **Flower Garland Buddhism** does relate individual things to other individual things. But Fa Tsang also relates all individual things to an underlying essence, a spiritual bottom line or foundation to the universe. Therefore many people argue that Flower Garland Buddhism is not Buddhism at all.

And if this is true, then most of East Asian "Buddhism"—Buddhism in China, Korea and Japan—is not really Buddhism at all, because much of it is based on the Flower Garland tendency to believe in an essence to the universe, out of which all things arise.

Alice: Well, what is this spiritual essence in Flower Garland Buddhism?

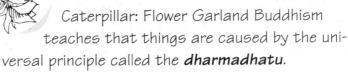

Caterpillar: Flower Garland Buddhism teaches that things are caused by the universal principle called the **dharmadhatu**.

Alice: What is the dharmadhatu?

Caterpillar: It is like an essence of the universe; a substratum, but a very unusual one. Because its nature is emptiness or void. You see the individual things of the universe really arise from themselves. So the universe arises from itself. But the things of the universe are empty and indivisible.

This indivisible emptiness is the True Nature of things. And rather than saying, like Nagarjuna's Madhyamika school, that even this emptiness of all things is empty—Poof!—Fa Tsang and his Flower Garland followers proclaim that Emptiness is the **true underlying nature of things, the real being or essence or foundation of the universe**.

For them Emptiness or the Void is like a entity. Like the emptiness inside of Lao Tzu's bowl. One must remember that Buddhism in China was in competition with Taoism, and had to transform itself in order to be accepted by the Chinese people. Also, the only way the Chinese could understand Buddhism was through their Taoist (or Confucian) lenses. So Buddhism became a little like Taoism and Confucianism.

Fa Tsang created a poetic image to titillate the senses of Empress Wu so that she would understand the doctrine of **interpenetration** and the nature of the dharmadhatu— the image of Indra's Net.

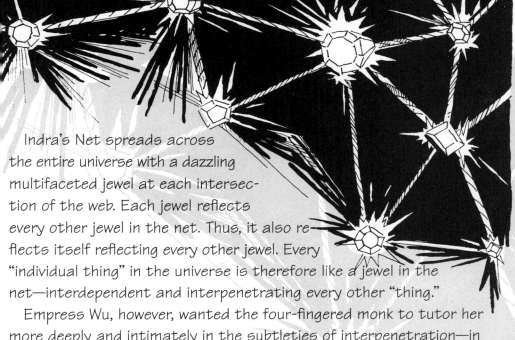

Indra's Net spreads across
the entire universe with a dazzling
multifaceted jewel at each intersec-
tion of the web. Each jewel reflects
every other jewel in the net. Thus, it also reflects itself reflecting every other jewel. Every
"individual thing" in the universe is therefore like a jewel in the
net—interdependent and interpenetrating every other "thing."

Empress Wu, however, wanted the four-fingered monk to tutor her
more deeply and intimately in the subtleties of interpenetration—in
a way that would appeal to her senses.

Fa Tsang told his Heavenly Empress Wu that he would satisfy her
desire. A few days later, he took Empress Wu by her delicate hand,
leading her into a huge multifaceted palace. Its many walls, ceiling,
and floor were completely covered with huge, shining mirrors, all facing one another at one angle or another.

"Tee hee" giggled the Empress! "This is one kinky monk! I can't wait
for his demonstration of interpenetration!"

Fa Tsang reached into his robe. He pulled out a statue of the
Buddha. He placed it in the center of the room. Then he placed a fu-
riously burning torch beside it. The Heavenly Empress opened her
eyes wide, wonderstruck, gazing into a phantasm of infinite inter-
reflections, each reflected and re-reflected in a dizzying dance of
inter-reflections.

Fa Tsang: Your Majesty! In each and every mirror you see the reflections of all the other mirrors, each with the Buddha's image in
them. And in each and every reflection you see all the reflections of all
the other mirrors, together with the specific Buddha image in each.

You see unveiled before you the mystery of interpenetration!

You see unveiled before you the mystery of one in all—and all in one.

You see unveiled before you the mystery of realm embracing realm.

You see unveiled before you the mystery of the simultaneous arising of different realms.

Caterpillar: He then took a crystal ball from his robe, placing it in the palm of his hand. All the mirrors and all their inter-reflections were now reflected in the one crystal ball.

Fa Tsang:

You now see unveiled before you the mystery of the small containing the large.

You also see unveiled before you the mystery of the large containing the small.

Caterpillar: Thus, there is no obstruction between sizes of realms, no obstruction between realms in space.

Empress Wu was impressed, and so were the Koreans, and the Japanese emperors who would come to favor this system of Buddhism. After all, the dharmadhatu is a **totalistic** system, with **everything arising from one point—the Buddha in the center**. This provided a perfect spiritual model for their totalitarian governments, with the emperor in the center, creating everything else.

Empress Wu was so pleased that she often called the good monk Fa Tsang from his translations of Sanskrit texts so that he could pray that her enemies would be swiftly killed.

Alice: How wicked! Was Flower Garland China's most popular form of Buddhism?

Caterpillar: No. **Pure Land Buddhism** and *Ch'an Buddhism* were eventually the most popular forms.

Pure Land Buddhism

Caterpillar: **Sukhavati**, the Pure and Happy Land, Western Paradise, is a Heaven. Gods and men inhabit this rich, fertile, and comfortable realm free of the temptations and defilements of earthly existence: animals, ghosts, devils, and women. Adorned with fragrant jeweled trees, It is filled with ponds of giant lotus blossoms and terraces with awe-inspiring panoramas, gleaming thrones and heavenly chimes. Through it flow rivers of sweetly scented waters, whose gentle banks grow scented jewel trees. The flowing waters of these rivers exude pleasant-sounding music that blends with the singing of heavenly birds and the melodious strains of celestial musicians. In the ears of beings dwelling there, this music transforms itself into the teachings of the Buddha.

Heavenly beings play and sport in waters that turn warm or cool at their slightest whim. And whatever the inhabitants wish, they receive instantly. Especially is their wish granted if they wish to attain Nirvana.

To attain this Pure Land, a believer needs not meditate till she turns blue in the face, nor does she have to be able to comprehend abstract and complex Buddhist doctrines such as Indra's Net. In fact, she doesn't have to understand anything at all, even if she had fallen to the state of a murderer such as Empress Wu. All she needs to do in her entire lifetime is to think, on her deathbed, of the name of the Buddha who presides over this Western Paradise—**Amita**. And Amita Buddha will beam her up!

It is easy to see how Pure Land Buddhism became the most popular form of Buddhism in China. In fact, it practically defined Chinese Buddhism, especially among the masses.

Thus, the simple invocation of Amitaba's name (O-mi-t'o-fo in Chinese) became the most popular religious practice in all of China. O-mi-t'o-fo is how the Chinese mispronounce the Sanskrit term Amitayur Buddha, the Buddha Who Possesses Infinite Life. In fact, the Chinese did not know the meaning of the sound, but this only added to its mystery. When they chanted "O-mi-t'o-fo" they found it exotic and mystical to intone a sound they could not understand, a sound from the exotic West (India!). Thus it became a magical spell, such as "abracadabra" is to us.

You don't need to be a great intellectual to worship a statue of the Buddha, or to chant "*O-mi-t'o-fo*." And, in fact, the Pure Land School of Buddhism taught that we now live in a fallen age in which Buddhist philosophy has degenerated into complex philosophical quarrels among various Buddhist scholars.

The quickest way to gain Nirvana in such an age is simply to abandon philosophy and worship **Amitaba**, seated on his Lotus Throne in his Western Paradise. And just as Christian devotees eventually developed a cult of devotion to the feminine aspect of God as found in Mary, Pure Land Buddhists, over time, increasingly worshipped **Kuan-Yin**, the Goddess of Mercy. Clad in white, she is a Bodhisattva who stands at the side of Amitaba calling the devout to the Western Paradise.

She soon became a popular household Goddess, **Sung-tzu kuan-yin**, the Giver of Children, worshipped by women all over China, whether Buddhist or not.

Eventually, Pure Land Buddhism spread to Japan, where it became a major sect.

Alice: But it doesn't appear that Pure Land Buddhism is very Buddhist either.

Caterpillar: You are right. It made the Buddha into a god. But the Buddha, himself, was totally unconcerned with gods. Luckily, **Ch'an** Buddhism came along to restore to Buddhism something of its original nature.

Ch'an Buddhism

Caterpillar: The practical Chinese eventually tired of all the intellectualism, ritual, and pomp of the other schools.

They wanted a practical way to enter the very **heart** of Buddhism, and they found that way in **Ch'an**: meditation. Ch'an is the way the Chinese mispronounce the Sanskrit word **dhyana** which means "meditation." (**Zen** is the way the Japanese mispronounce **Ch'an**—and Zen is the Japanese version of Ch'an.) During the T'ang, the Chinese love of practicality and the world led them to accept C'han Buddhism. Ch'an was originally brought to China by a Buddhist monk from Persia. His name was **Bodhidharma**. Soon two warring schools of Ch'an formed: the Northern School, teaching that enlightenment is a gradual process, and the Southern School, teaching a doctrine of Sudden Enlightenment. The Southern School gained popularity among the masses and the elite. It eventually displaced the Northern school.

The first great master of the Southern School was **Huineng**. He became the Sixth Patriarch of Ch'an, even though he had been only a humble rice-pounder in the monastery kitchen.

Legend has it that the head monk of the monastery, and founder of the Northern School of Ch'an had written the following poem:

The body is the tree of enlightenment;
The mind is the stand of a bright mirror.
At all times diligently wipe it clean.
Do not allow it to become dirty.

Huineng responded with the following poem:

> **Enlightenment is not a tree;**
> **Nor is the mind a mirror stand.**
> **Since originally there was nothing,**
> **Where would the dust fall?**

The Fifth Patriarch of Ch'an recognized Huineng's genius, and gave him his robe—thus making him the Sixth Patriarch.

Alice: What did Huineng teach?

Caterpillar: Huineng taught one thing: Practice no-thought!

He knew that enlightenment cannot be grasped by thought—by thinking about it. Thus, in meditation, be no-thought.

Caterpillar: Like the Taoists, Ch'an masters taught freedom and spontaneity. They were also iconoclasts: "Kill everything that stands in your way. If you meet the Buddha, kill the Buddha!"

Still other Ch'an masters resorted to a kind of shock therapy, by giving irrational answers to questions:

Monk: Who is the Buddha?
Master: Three pounds of flax.

Huineng: Neither the flag nor the wind is moving—only your minds.

133

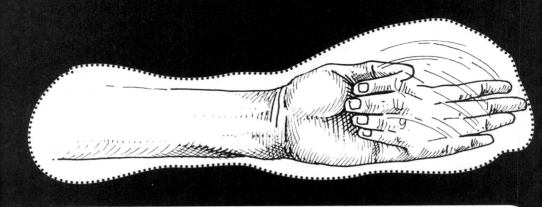

Caterpillar: Other Ch'an teachers would ask their monks to meditate on riddles such as, "What is the sound of one hand clapping?"

Of course, the intellect cannot give an answer, so the monk is
thus forced to rely upon his intuition.

Such riddles came to be known as Kung-an—or problems—and
many a Ch'an monk has spent years cracking his head against one.

Alice: Well, if Ch'an and Pure Land were the most popular schools
of Buddhism, which schools were the minor ones?

The Three Treatise (San-Lun) School

Caterpillar: **The Three Treatise School** is simply the Chinese
incarnation of India's **Madhyamika** school. It is known as the
Three Treatise School because of three important scriptures:
Treatise on the Middle Way, *Treatise in One Hundred Verses*,
and *Treatise on the Twelve Gates*. It was **Kumarajiva** who
translated these into Chinese, thus bringing Nagarjuna's notions of Emptiness to China. And the Chinese were already
pre-programmed to accept this notion. For one thing, Lao Tzu,
the great-granddaddy of Taoism, had prepared the Chinese for
the idea of Emptiness by praising Emptiness as a quality of
the Tao. The Tao is empty, like a bowl. But of course, Lao Tzu's
concept of Emptiness was quite different from Nagarjuna's.

Another feature of Nagarjuna's thought that appealed to the family-oriented Chinese was its emphasis that reality has something to do with relations between things, not to some underlying reality. Things exist only in their dependent relationship to other things. Thus, they both exist and do not exist. They exist like the grains of rice in a begging bowl that a magician has transformed by an illusion to look like flies! While in reality, the flies do not exist, they still exist as an illusion.

In fact, in reality there is no difference between the "flies" and the grains of rice. Like that, there is no difference between the seemingly separate and real "things" of the world, and ultimate Emptiness.

There is no difference between the world and Nirvana! This is another Madhyamika idea that the Chinese found appealing.

The Consciousness Only (Fa hsiang) School

Caterpillar: **The School of Consciousness Only** was the Chinese version of the **Vijnanavada** or **Yogachara** school of Indian Buddhism. The great Chinese teacher of this school is **Hsuan-tsang**. His version is known as the **Dharma Characteristics School**. Hsuan-tsang made an epic journey from China to central Asia and India from where he brought back dozens of Buddhist scriptures, translating them into Chinese.

Like its Indian version, the Chinese school taught that the mind stands between the senses and the storehouse of impressions. When we perceive objects through our senses, then our experiences are stored in our storehouse of impressions—in seed form. But these seeds influence the way in which we will perceive and experience new objects. Thus, a seed produces a manifestation and a manifestation produces a seed. Cause and effect are one and the same.

But, in the end, the hairsplitting analyses and far-out terminology of this school were too difficult and abstract for the worldly-minded Chinese.

SURE, AS LONG AS MY PLANE GOTS TWO.

The Lotus (T'ien-tai) School

Caterpillar: As a mere child, **Chih-i** began displaying spectacular talents. Closing his eyelids, he could envision events that had taken place in the far past. Upon first hearing a group of monks chanting a **sutra**, he would then repeat the entire sutra, himself. He embraced a monastic life, withdrawing to Mount T'ien-t'ai, where he developed China's first system of Buddhist thought, named after the mountain on which he taught. His meditation manual, **"T'ung-meng chich-kuan"** or *"Meditation for Beginners,"* is still a classic.

Being a Southerner with a teacher from the North, one of Chih-i's great tasks was to discover a middle ground between Southern

Chinese intellectual Buddhism and the Northern Chinese contemplative approach. Contemplating this problem, he asked himself: "Can a bird fly with only one wing?"

Thus, his **T'ien-t'ai** school is steeped in **both** deep meditation and in much philosophy.

Alice: What was the philosophy?

Caterpillar: Chih-i taught three levels of truth:

▶ All things (**dharmas**) are empty (**shunyata**) of self-nature, because they are caused.

▶ However, they *do* appear to have a temporary existence (kind of like bubbles).

▶ All things (dharmas) are BOTH temporary *and* empty—and this is the MEAN!

All three of the above levels of truth involve and embrace each other. In the Truth Realm of Temporariness there are Ten Worlds, the worlds of:

1 beings in hell
2 hungry ghosts
3 beasts
4 fighting demons
5 men
6 heavenly beings
7 direct disciples of the Buddha
8 private Buddhas
9 Bodhisattvas
10 Buddha

But each of these 10 worlds interpenetrates all the others, so that there are 100 temporary realms! Thus, Buddhahood is possible for beings in Hell, and it is possible for a Buddha to get a headache or go to Hell! No being is absolutely good or evil. All these temporary realms interpenetrate each other like soap bubbles in a washing machine—and are empty of self-existence. Thus, any being anywhere can realize Emptiness.

Alice: And what about their practices?

Caterpillar: Chih-i founded his school on the Lotus Sutra, a scripture from India teaching the way of the Bodhisattva. Therefore a major Tien-t'ai practice is helping other beings—because that is what Bodhisattvas do, since they believe we are all interconnected!

Another practice is the meditation method known as **chih-kuan**. This teaches that the mind is like a lake. **Chih** is the still mental lake. And **kuan** is the insight of **shunyata** or lack of forms reflected by this still mind. After the Chi-

nese had reflected on it for awhile, Tien-t'ai traveled East to become a major school of Japanese Buddhism.

After the T'ang Dynasty, Buddhism went into a tailspin. Pure Land Buddhism and Ch'an, however, survived, and even flourished. For one thing they didn't rely so much on external forms of religion-upon scriptures, temples, states, and Buddhist art. So when these were burned by Confucian fanatics, they were not affected. In fact, the Ch'an Buddhists often burned scriptures and statues of the Buddha just to demonstrate that they didn't depend upon them, or perhaps just to keep their hands warm. Also, Ch'an had a strong following in the provinces, far away from the politics of the cities.

Alice: So, it was the Confucianists that pushed the Buddhists aside?

Caterpillar: Actually, it was Neo-Confucianists.

THE NEO-CONFUCIAN REVIVAL

For nearly eight centuries, from the decline of the Han Dynasty (220 A.D.) until the ascent of the Sung Dynasty (960 A.D.), Buddhism captivated the Chinese. Scholars all over China and from as far as India, Persia, Korea, and Japan traveled to China's famous Buddhist temples for learning. At times China's rulers showered support upon these temples, the illustrious monks who taught in them, and commissioned great Buddhist works of art in painting, sculpture, and architecture.

Relationships between people at home and at the office still conformed to an ingrained Confucian sense of "oughtness." But the main reason that Confucianism did not disappear entirely during these centuries was the civil service exams, based on the **Confucian Classics**.

The typical young scholar roamed in his mind through the forest of the **Confucian Classics.** He hunted for a metaphor through sensuous poetic images, gentle and graceful odes, convincing essays, elegies painful and tangled, and songs devoted to ancestors, singing the clean fragrance of their virtue. He was, after all, taking the civil service exam.

Founded in the Han Dynasty, expanded under the T'ang, and reaching their climax during the Sung, the exams were held every three years, offering talented scholars the chance to rise to positions of honor and authority.

The entire future of the young scholar depended on how dazzling his metaphors were, how precise and convincing his arguments, how elegant and balanced his style, how rhythmic his cadences, how fine his distinctions, how powerful his central phrase. Pulling upon his sparse beard, he snared an obscure line, neglected by generations of scholars, illumining its complex darkness until it seemed simple. Responding to ancient conventions and laws of composition, his lines flowed like water in a river, like silk pulled from a cocoon.

On these he would be judged, for if his essays were successful he would enter public office. Theoretically, if he had meditated well on the writings of the ancients, he might become a model for all men, his speeches might help salvage a sinking branch of government, his military odes—brilliant as shining jade veins in a mountain of bureaucratic prose—might inspire an entire army to victory.

In reality, between exams he would probably steal off with his fellow students to the mountain tea plantations at night. There they would stuff their book bags with stolen tea leaves, smuggle them back to the city, and sell them for profit. If, on the way, they got caught in the rain, they would scream about drowning in a flood. If the road was hot, they would proclaim it a drought, all the time cracking "Confucius say..." jokes, and deliberately misquoting Mencius!

Such was the spell that Confucian scholarship cast over scholarly minds, even during the full blossoming of Buddhism. It could have been only a matter of time, then, that native Confucian this-worldliness with its sense of social responsibility reasserted itself, revolting against Buddhism's otherworldliness, and pushing it to the background.

Han Yu

The first evidence of this tendency appeared as early as the T'ang Dynasty (786-824 A.D.). **Han Yu** adopted an ancient prose style, quoting the maxims of the ancient masters to defend Confucian principles, with an energy and strictness not seen since Mencius.

> *"Buddhism is nothing more than a cult spread in China by barbarians!"* —Han Yu

Han Yu boldly attacked the ruler for ordering a community of Buddhist monks to piously greet a bone, supposedly belonging to the Buddha, as it was being ceremoniously brought into the palace where it would be permanently worshipped.

Hu Yuan

Another Neo-Confucian philosopher, **Hu Yuan**, believed that too conventional an education and too much dependence on scholarship could only mean repeating the past, producing Confucian scholars blander than cabbage broth, thinner than the notes from a temple lute—elegant and literary—but without true gristle. Hu Yuan advocated a return to a strong teacher-disciple relationship, in the manner of Confucius and his students. He wanted to apply Confucian values to contemporary life.

WOULD YOU RATHER NOTHING WAS SACRED?

141

Chang Tsai

Imagine a landscape painting from the Sung Dynasty, the era in which **Chang Tsai** (1020-1077), wrote. Jagged mountain peaks and roiling rivers

loom into view, emerging from the pearly light of clouds or floating atop celestial oceans of mist, into which they seem to disappear and then reappear like ephemeral islets. The viewer is left with the impression that mountain and cloud, form and emptiness, are only eternally interweaving currents of energy. The most adamant mountain erodes according to its geological nature as surely as any cloud does according to its meteorological laws.

The Chinese saw in this dreamworld of interweaving energy patterns an ocean surging with tidal forces. This ocean of the universe is composed of **Ch'i,** "breath" or "energy." Ch'i constantly solidifies or dissolves, warms or cools, rises or falls, ebbs or flows between two poles of energy.

One pole—feminine, abysmal, passive, shadowy, moist, and symbolized by cloud, mist, valley, winter, and midnight—is called Yin. The other pole— masculine, vigorous, active, sunlit, dry, and symbolized by mountain peak, constellation, summer, and noon—is called Yang. Everything is always Yin-ing or Yang-ing. With the fierce, Yang heat of noon, a turning point is reached, and the Yin begins to grow in proportion to Yang until it reaches its maximum, and another turning point, at midnight. Movement and stillness, hardness and softness—all pairs—alternate between Yin and Yang.

Chang Tsai believed that since all things are made up of this primordial energy, called Ch'i, all things are harmoniously linked:

"Heaven is my Father. Earth is my mother. All people are my brothers and sisters."

This was called the **Western Inscription**, because he wrote it on a wall. It took the traditional Confucian emphasis on family, and re-formed it to include everyone and everything. All the crippled, maimed and ill, deformed and lonely are brothers and sisters. If one protects them, then one is showing the Confucian reverence of a son. This attitude extended the reach of Jen, or human kindness, beyond the family, and had a tremendous influence on subsequent Confucian thought. His teachings were based on the I Ching.

The Brothers Cheng

Cheng Hao (1032-1085) and **Cheng Yi** (1033-1107) both drew upon the notion of Chang Tsai that the universe is made up of Ch'i.

They argued, however, that Ch'i is only the raw material, the basic goop, of the universe. To this they added the concept of Li.

Li is the **Eternal Principle** or law(s) which mold the basic stuff of the Ch'i into individual things. Nothing can come into manifestation without Li to give it form. Moreover, they both advocated the study of Li, or Ultimate Principle, which they saw as identical with **human nature**. Yet, Cheng Yi's emphasis was on **investigation of external things,** for even trees and grass contain Li. This gave rise to **The School of Laws.**

Cheng Hao, on the other hand, emphasized **developing the inner life of the mind**, giving rise to **The School of Mind**. They both taught that one should study *Li*, the **Ultimate Principle**, because it is one with human nature. By developing one's own nature, one can act in accordance with Li. They both emphasized the cultivation of Jen, or human kindness, since all beings are just different forms of Ch'i.

They both taught that by seriousness or sincerity, inner and outer life can be united harmoniously.

Chu Tzu (The School Of Laws)

As soft breezes trembled through his silken robe, **Chu Tzu** lectured to China's most illustrious philosophers, all gathered at his Academy of the White Deer.

Alice: What did he lecture on?

Caterpillar: White butterflies dancing among pear blossoms, white lotus flowers trembling upon clear waters, white clouds shifting shapes in the wind, pearly moonlight dancing in thousands of lakes and rivers. But for the sage Chu Tzu, these were not Buddhist images suggesting the world's Emptiness. In fact, Chu Tzu attacked Buddhists with the force of a typhoon felling a forest. Rather, these were Confucian images, for Chu Tzu was a Neo-Confucian, drawing upon the thought of Cheng Yi. The school he founded bore both of their names. Called the **Cheng-Chu School** or **School of Principles**, it became the most prominent Neo-Confucian school, making Chu Tzu the most influential Chinese thinker after Confucius. Moreover, his thought would dominate China from the 12th until the 20th century, when China would encounter Western thought.

Alice: Well if not Emptiness, what did Chu Tzu see in the butterflies?

Caterpillar: According to Chu Tzu, everything in this **real** universe—butterflies, lotuses, clouds, and moonlight—is made up of Li (principle, pattern, structure, idea) and Ch'i (primordial material force). This much he had borrowed from the brothers Cheng.

Li is the Universal Pattern. It is the butterfly-*ness* that all types of butterflies share; the cloud-*ness* that the billowing thundercloud, the nimbostratus, the cirrus, and the altocumulus share; the lotus-*ness* common to blue, black, purple, or white lotus blossoms.

Ch'i, on the other hand, is the stuff which makes individual expressions of universal Li possible. Ch'i makes each individual butterfly, snow petal, flying pear blossom, every little cloud of willow or cottonwood fluff dancing the wind, **unique**. One blossom may be full-bodied and fragrant, another pale and odorless, depending upon different qualities of Ch'i.

Alice: Isn't that like Plato, who argued for Ideal Forms, which exist independently of their objects?

Caterpillar: Well, no. Because **Li cannot exist independently from Ch'i** anymore than the reflections of the moonlight in thousands of rivers and lakes can exist apart from the moon.

Alice: Is there one **great** Li or principle that contains *all* the different Li's and Chi's in the universe?

Caterpillar: Yes, and Chu Tzu called this the ***T'ai chi*** or the **Great Ultimate**.

Alice: Well, how can this exist in everything in the universe?

Chu Tzu: "The full moon, floating across boundless space, its golden light dancing in thousands of lakes and rivers, is yet never divided."

Alice: I see! The moon is not like a huge stained glass window that gets smashed and falls in the ocean.

How can I know this supreme Li, this T'ai chi or Great Ultimate?

Chu Tzu: In order to become a morally superior person one must recognize the Li that nature has already put inside of you. And the best way to accomplish this is through the investigation of things: butterflies, clouds, human relationships, political problems, etc. Since the Li in human nature is the same as the Li's in the rest of nature, if we investigate into things, then we can attune ourselves to Li.

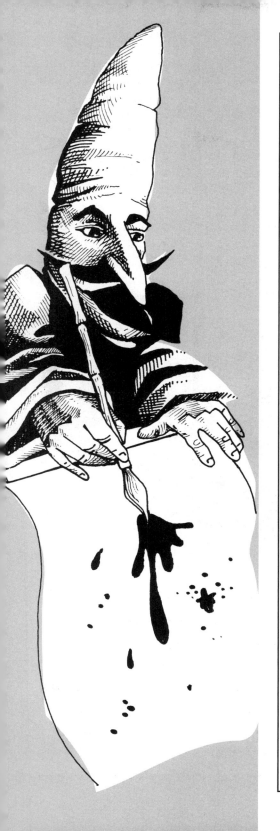

Caterpillar: Of course, according to Chu Tzu, the best place to learn of the nature of this is the **Classics**. Thus, Chu Tzu is famous for editing and writing original commentaries on what he called the **Four Books**:

- *The Analects (of Confucius)*
- *The Book of Mencius*
- *The Doctrine of the Mean*
- *The Great Learning.*

Lu Hsiang-shan (The School of Mind)

Caterpillar: **Lu Hsiang-shan** challenged Chu Tzu's views, completing Cheng Hao's **School of Mind**. Whereas Chu Tzu had made fine distinctions between **Li** (the inner nature of things) and **Ch'i** (the nature of embodied beings), between human nature and minds, Lu Hsiang-shan (1130-1192), showed that **all of these are just Mind**. Mind is Li. Mind is the universe. And since humans already possess Mind, then there is no real need to investigate into the principles of things, in the external world, nor in the **Classics**, since it is all in the Mind.

Lu Hsiang-shan: "There is only one mind. My friend's mind, the mind of the sages thousands of years ago, and the mind of the sages thousands of years to come are all the same. The substance of the mind is infinite. If one can completely develop his mind, he will become identical with Heaven. Turn within!" *

For century after century Chinese civilization had patterned its society on the vision of an ideal past, and the practice of administering the government by a civil service made up of classical scholars. If the West had not intruded, it is possible that traditional Chinese civilization might well have continued as it had for thousands of years. However, the West did intrude. Western commercial incursions into China developed with the shipment of sandalwood and ginseng. The Portuguese in the 16th century, and the Dutch in the 17th century, had traded along the Chinese coast. The Chinese had, for the most part, been able to handle these Western encounters on its own terms. But when the British began busying themselves smuggling Indian opium into China, the Chinese reacted.

In 1839, the Chinese informed Queen Victoria that her barbarian ships were smuggling opium to all the provinces in order to poison the Chinese peoples for the profit of the English. The letter proclaimed that China only exported silk, tea, woolens, and other beneficial materials. Therefore, all Chinese and English caught trafficking in opium would be summarily executed.

The British invaded, starting the Opium War. The Chinese, who for centuries had felt somewhat invincible, were overwhelmed by Britain's superior military might. When the Opium War ended, with the signing of the Treaty of Nanking, the British had gained the right to trade openly in China, and they even got Hong Kong thrown in as part of the bargain.

Even though China was opening up to trade, nearly all Chinese people remained suspicious of the Western barbarians who were constantly eating away at her culture and humiliating her. But a new attitude began to develop: the attitude that the foreign barbarians had something worthwhile to contribute to Chinese culture and that China could actually learn something from the barbarians.

One thing was certain, however: the traditional scholar-officials were no longer trusted. What had they done to fend off the barbarians? And what had they contributed in the effort to modernize China?

One of the things that China began learning from the West was religion. The foreign devils had received from the Chinese the right to spread the Word of God. Christian missionaries brought a message from their Heavenly Father. The message was of divine love, salvation, and life eternal, all backed up by Western gunboats. Mostly, the unlettered peasants took to the new religion—or at least took advantage of its schools, hospitals, and rice.

SEE, MOM, A BROTHER! AND WHY DID HE GET TO HAVE HIS KINGDOM ON EARTH, POP?

One rebel leader, attempting to overthrow the Manchu rulers, even created his own version of Christianity. His name was **Hung Shiu-ch'uan**, and he proclaimed himself Heavenly King, revising the New Testament to say that he was the Divine Younger Brother of Jesus Christ. Millions of Chinese accepted his branch of Christianity. They were told that they would go to Heaven if they died while fighting for him, giving rise to the **Taiping Rebellion**.

After defeating the imperial forces, he established himself in Nanking, surrounded with his 68 wives, 300 male attendants, and devout followers. He preached the equality of men and women, and the value of education and social welfare. He banned opium smoking, foot-binding, prostitution, slavery, and ancestor-worship. Then, when his power began to wane, he committed suicide.

149

The Winter Period (1912-?)

Sun Yat-sen

At night, dragons and snakes tangled their dreams. During the day, thoughts of the suffering masses stirred their minds, they raised their voices to call for a people's democracy, and vowed no more to bow their heads to serve the Emperor. None of this could have happened without the philosophical genius of **Sun Yat-sen** (1866-1926), a thinker who was also a politician. Therefore, he emphasized action-political action. His boyhood hero, after all, had been Hung Shiu-ch'uan, the leader of the Taiping Rebellion.

Educated almost entirely in Western schools, Sun was so impressed with the democracies of Europe and the United States that he began to envision democracy as the political philosophy capable of bringing China into the modern world. This would mean, of course, that government would have to pass from the hands of the few into the hands of the many.

Although Sun believed people were born with different talents and abilities, he felt that everyone should be given an opportunity to develop their full potential without interference from society. His vision of democracy for China was based on the "Five-Power Democratic System." Like American democracy, it relied upon an executive, a legislative, and a judicial branch. But to these Sun added two more branches: the examination branch and the supervision branch. Both of these were modern expressions of traditional Chinese institutions.

AWAKE!

Sun also envisioned a program of land reform. The government would buy the land from the wealthy landowners and then give it back to the farmers. In order to do all of this he emphasized **action**. His message fired the spirits of Chinese youth, who took up arms in order to realize his "Three Principles of the People:"

NATIONALISM
DEMOCRACY
ECONOMICS.

Though they enjoyed some military and political success in China, these were short-lived. In time, their tears would flow like silken threads and swell into a red tide. Sun died, and his nationalist Army was defeated by Mao's Red Army. It was only in Taiwan that Sun's followers were able to implement a modern democracy along the lines he had envisioned.

MAO TSE-TUNG

A threatening sea of flags and banners surged at the foot of the mountain. Bugle calls and drum rolls echoed from valley to valley. Tightly encircled by Nationalist forces, the Red Army remained hidden deep within the mists of Chinkan Mountain.

Chinkan Mountain was the cradle of the Chinese Communist Revolution, a summit of rugged terrain, dense fog, and luxuriant forests of pine and bamboo where the young **Mao** (1893-1976) hid away, and composed his bold and imaginative poetry. In doing so, he was able to tap into the mystique of the hidden rebel-sage-poet, and thus inspire the population to rise in his defense like a red sea.

But Mao called for a kind of revolution different from any that China had experienced before. Although the son of a peasant, with a deep understanding of the predominantly rural population of China, he began to read Russian Marxist texts in the 1930s. This led him to invent his own version of Chinese Marxism, which under the Chinese Communist Party, and the People's Republic of China, would revolutionize China and influence the rest of the world.

Mao's philosophy, drawing upon Hegel, Marx, Engels, Lenin, Stalin, and Taoism taught that all things are **material**, **real**, and **interconnected**. Also, everything has contradiction deep within itself. Thus, contradiction is a major Maoist concept. Any argument, riot, or what we would call an issue involves contradiction.

According to the **Law of the Unity of Opposites**, the two parts of any contradiction are **interdependent**. In Mao's words, "Everything divides in two."

Additionally, Mao taught that most things involve many contradictions, but there is always a **central** one. For instance, a couple may bicker about a million little things, but never get down to the real issue, which is the central contradiction.

Within this central contradiction, one of two elements will dominate the other. For instance, in capitalist societies, the class with the capital is dominant, while the working class is the underdog. Therefore, Mao taught that we must understand contradiction, so that we can bring about a reversal, thus allowing the underdog to gain dominance.

But all this philosophy, which he explained in *On Contradiction*, was worth nothing without action. Therefore he wrote *Guerrilla Warfare* and *On Practice* to emphasize the importance of political action to bring about real change in both the inner and outer worlds.

As Mao demonstrated in his own poetry, the role of art and literature in a Maoist society is important: it should inspire the people. In the visual arts the results can be seen on posters all over China, and even on the currency. Pull a **yuan** note from your wallet, and you will find por-traits of heroically smiling Chinese workers. The official image of the socialist hero, after all, is one of an active, productive healthy citizen who toils smilingly, and without any philosophical hesitations about his role in society. He welcomes personal sacrifice as a way of building a truly socialist world. Set these ideas to music, and you have something of a cross between a march and a symphony, dedicated to reforming the hearts and minds of workers, to reeducating them in the spirit of self-sacrifice. All this adds up to an art which inspires workers to toil, and to toil happily, for the good of all. The freedom of the artist to depict life as he or she sees it is subordinate to the artistic need to inspire society to advance steadily towards its socialist goals. The musician, like the writer and painter, is expected to sacrifice personal truth to social ideals (a very Confucian notion). This idea, of course, formed the justification of the **Cultural Revolution,** and the death or imprisonment of many artists, intellectuals, and scholars.

Mao: "What's so unusual about Emperor Shih Huang of the Chin Dynasty? He had buried alive 460 scholars only, but we have buried alive 46,000 scholars. . . . We are 100 times ahead of Emperor Shih of the Chin Dynasty in repression of Counter-revolutionary scholars."

THE UNBEARABLE LIGHTNESS OF BEIJING

Alice: But if China is no longer truly Maoist, then what is it? Has any major thinker replaced Mao?

Caterpillar: No major thinker has come along, but the Chinese do dream about things Western: democracy, capitalism, rock and roll. In fact rock, for a while was a political and philosophical force.

In 1986, you could stuff all the rockers in China into a rickshaw. For three decades prior to that, the music industry had been in the hands of the government. But in the 1980s, the state-operated music industry became open to outside influence. After toiling happily all week, it actually became possible for Chinese workers suffering from Saturday night fever to file into discos and dance to songs extolling the bliss of productivity. As the evening wore on, lovers would clutch their partners, and slow-dance to syrupy Chinese love songs imported from Taiwan or Hong Kong.

It was only around 1986 that **Cui Jan**, who was to become something of the Elvis of China, got his hands on some Beatles and Stones tapes. These only whetted his appetite for more potent fare. He was soon devouring Bob Marley, the Police, the Clash—anything he could get his hands on.

THE GLORIOUS PEASANTRY WILL FOREVER FURTHER THE RIGHTEOUS REVOLUTION FLATTENING AND BURYING THE ROSES OF BOURGEOIS SEDUCTION BY BLAH, BLAH, BLAH, BLAH...

Soon a network of underground clubs sprang up like mushrooms, playing black-market tapes of Led Zeppelin, Pink Floyd, Rush, and other, more subversive Western bands. Chinese students returning home from study abroad were not only bringing back Western rock, they also brought with them authors like Kundera, Solzhenitsyn, and Milosz.

In 1986, when Cui Jian performed at a pop music contest in Beijing, singing lyrics that could have landed him in prison, he brought the stunned crowd to their feet. It didn't take long for the government to brand him a criminal and ban him from recording or performing.

Just before the massacre in Tiananmen Square, the ban was lifted. In 1988, the state-run record company released Cui Jian's first album, *New Long March Rock*. It was to become the soundtrack for the Tiananmen movement. In March of 1989, he played two packed stadium concerts to college crowds in Beijing. His music was becoming a socio-political force.

Little more than a month later the Beijing students took to the streets, erected a statue of the Goddess of Democracy, and came close to toppling the government. On the night of June 3rd, however, tanks, artillery, and trucks carrying soldiers rolled into the square. By the time it was all over, an estimated 1,000 were dead.

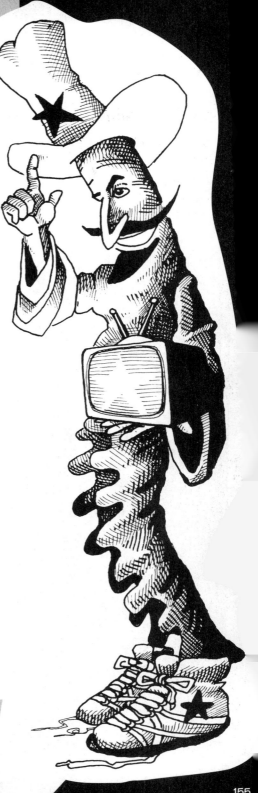

After the slaughter in Tiananmen, the government began compiling lists of rock artists. Playing a concert could get a musician arrested. Understandably, rock went underground again, becoming something to be enjoyed only by China's bohemian set—students, artists, foreigners—in shadowy underground venues in Beijing. For many years, rock was barred from radio and television, and artists were only allowed to hold small concerts. Many artists simply left the city.

These days rock is no longer illegal in China, as long as the lyrics aren't critical of Beijing. But that isn't the full story. Under the directives of economic reform, the state-owned record companies must suddenly turn a profit. Capitalism is replacing socialism. As a result, some rockers, while still banned from playing, nevertheless began recording with the state-run companies. Their CDs began being distributed in state-run stores. After all, both rockers and Beijing had to face certain realities.

Beijing realized that if they wanted the state-run record industry to turn a profit, they needed to give the masses something appealing. Rockers simply realized that it is dangerous, and therefore stupid, to perform a song which is politically offensive. Most have discovered that the real money is to be made by recording sappy love songs. China's leading heavy metal band, **Tang Dynasty**, eschews political lyrics, instead creating fantasies of a return to ancient Chinese civilization.

But the Beijing government is not the only enemy of raw, politically inspired rock in China. The biggest foe is the Chinese people, the masses of workers themselves. They work hard. Many of the young people work at three or four jobs. They view the fashion, hairdos, and lifestyles of rockers as irrelevant, something for an elite core of individuals who have the luxury of leisure. Besides, most workers would rather enjoy a night of karaoke or disco than get all riled up over the lyrics of some angry rocker. Musically then, one-quarter of the world's population is listening to Canto Pop, soft Chinese rock.

Go to Xiamen's ultra-modern new airport. In the seats next to you will sit Japanese and German businessmen, Taiwanese tourists, Tibetan tribesmen, and Chinese bureaucrats. Above you, as luminous as Mao's moonlike face, and held aloft by stainless steel columns, glow gigantic television monitors. And you can sit there for hours, transfixed, enthralled, eyes glued to the Chinese version of MTV, a mix of syrupy Canto-Pop and American and British lite-rock. Then you will realize, the philosopher who has replaced Mao is nothing more than a mix of capitalism, technology, and American popular culture. The Beijing government calls it "Socialism Chinese Style." They might better have named it "The Unbearable Lite-ness of Beijing."

THE PHILOSOPHIES AND RELIGIONS OF JAPAN

White mists hover over still waters. The blade of your canoe paddle flashes and plunges. With a thud, the prow strikes shore. Pine needles on the bank. You pull the canoe half up out of the water. Fallen, rotting trees nurse fungi, lichen, moss, and saplings. Before you the forest looms green, somber, cool, mute. Branches interlace. Towering crowns, dense with red cones. A slanting ray of light illumines one trunk-a giant, golden column. Radiant it stands, calm, eternal. Words mean nothing in front of this fir. Silently, it refuses names, descriptions, thought. In its stillness you learn to listen. To whisper. To touch. To feel.

Shinto
(The Way of the Gods)

Sacred shrines in **Shinto**—Japan's earliest religion—were simply spaces in which to feel awe. They were open spaces in a forest, containing a single, awe-inspiring pine or boulder that was possessed with awesome power. A mountain peak, a river, the sea, birds, deer, foxes, emperors, ancestors, and heroes could also be awe-inspiring. Usually, the awe-inspiring rock or tree was enclosed in a shrine. To enter the sacred space, you walked through a kind of gate known as a **torii**. Someteimes a torii was simply placed before a view of a mountain or bay, framing it, as if to say: "Stop! Listen! Feel! Things are awesome!"

All of these awe-inspiring rocks, trees, peaks, rivers, bays, and forests are called **kami**.

Alice: Kami?

Caterpillar: Kami is anything that inspires the emotion of awe. And just about anything inspires awe, as everything is a manifestation of Spirit. But there are not only earthly kami, but also heavenly, divine kami. Shinto, after all, means "way of the Gods." Shinto myths are collected in two books: the Kenjiki and the Nihongi. These myths tell of two kami, **Izanagi** and **Izanami**, who created the world. The myths also tell of the most powerful kami of all: **Amaterasu**, the **Sun Goddess**. She was born from the left eye of the primordial kami, Izanagi.

Her brother treated her badly, so she hid in the cave of heaven, closing the entrance with an enormous stone. Darkness engulfed the world, and evil spirits flew up out of their hiding places, carrying on their mischief everywhere. The Gods held a conference. They decided to lure Amaterasu from her cave by throwing a wild party. They placed a huge mirror in front of the cave, and placed resplendent jewels on a tree. **Yzume, Goddess of Laughter**, began dancing to the drums. Amaterasu, enchanted by the exotic music and laughter, could not resist. She took a peek. Instantly she saw her own brilliant reflection shining resplendently in the mirror. She came out of the cave, covering and coloring the world with light.

Alice: Where did Shinto come from?

Caterpillar: You could say that it came from the simple, pure, and spontaneous feeling of awe in the heart:

Gazing on Mount Fuji — overawed,
My head bows humbly of its own accord.

It comes from the innate feeling of the Japanese people for the pristine beauty of their beautiful islands.

Historically, however, the early Japanese were not a distinct nation as they are today. There were a conglomeration of different tribes, each inhabiting a fertile valley of their mountainous islands.

Their system of writing was called **Jindai-moji**, which predates Chinese writing, introduced only in the 3rd century. Their beliefs were a mix of local folklore, mixed in with currents of Polynesian culture, and Northern Asian Shamanism.

It was Shintoism that brought together in one religion the different currents of Shamanism, fertility rites and courtly festivals, myths, nature worship, ancestor worship, and the love of the Japanese for their single unbroken line of emperors of divine descent. Eventually Shinto provided a religious force that unified the Japanese nation.

Shinto has no scriptures or doctrines, but it does have shamans who supposedly possess magical powers to communicate with the kami.

Alice: What does Shinto mean?

Caterpillar: Shinto is from two Chinese characters. One is Shen, or "God," and the other is **Tao**, or "**Way**." So it means, the **Way of the Gods**.

Alice: Chinese character? But isn't Shinto Japanese?

Caterpillar: Yes, Shinto is a religion native to Japan. However, the Japanese borrowed the Chinese system of writing, starting in the 3rd century A.D. Thus it is from ancient Chinese histories that we learn about ancient Japan.

Beginning in the 6th Century, the Japanese began importing Chinese culture on a large scale. Some of the major   imports were Confucianism,
Buddhism, and Taoism—   which quickly developed
in ways uniquely   Japanese.

Shiungon Buddhism

Take **Shiungon** (**True Word**) **Buddhism**, for example. Brought back to Japan by **Kukai** (774-835 A.D.), it exemplifies the Japanese tendency to see ultimate reality in this very world. For Kukai, the awe-inspiring sound of the wind in the pines, of birdsong, or the koto are all preachings of the Buddha. The awe inspired by a beautiful painting is a sermon straight from the mouth of the Buddha. In fact, Kukai wrote a book on the subject: *On Becoming a Buddha Alive in the Human Body.*

Another tendency in Japanese religious thought derives from their Shamanistic past: a belief in the use of incantations, charms, and divinations. Thus, Kukai taught that the Buddha could be experienced by meditating upon his special sound or mantra. And although mantras are from India, the Japanese Shamanistic beliefs in chanting prepared them for this type of worship:

> **Chanting a sutra**
> **Suddenly, I am deeply blessed**
> **With morning glories, blooming loveliest.**

In fact, all the major Chinese Buddhist sects had their Japanese equivalents, but with a Japanese twist.

Zen Buddhism

Alice: In what ways did Ch'an Buddhism and Pure Land Buddhism change when they came to Japan?

Caterpillar: Actually, Ch'an Buddhism was declining in China, when it was brought to Japan, and renamed **Zen**.

Zen, of course, was perfect for the Japanese, because it proclaimed no difference between enlightenment and ordinary day-to-day activities. In Japan, Zen split into two different schools: **Renzai** and **Soto**. Renzai is famous for its reliance on dramatic meetings between a master and his disciple who has been meditating until blue in the face, upon a koan or Zen riddle such as "What is the sound of one hand clapping?"

If the disciple—in response to the question—pulls out a Ph.D. thesis, he flunks! However, if he tries to kick his master where it will really hurt, shout at him, or cut off his finger, this is evidence that he is making progress.

It was the famous master **Dogen** (1200-1253) who brought **Soto Zen** to Japan from China. Soto Zen emphasizes **silent** meditation and the identification of meditation itself with enlightenment. Dogen frequently wrote that the Buddha nature is the mountains, the river, the moon, the sound of the stream. Thus, he went beyond the assertion that all things **have** the Buddha nature. He said that all things **are** the Buddha nature.

It was Dogen who emphasized **Zazen**—just sitting.

Try it for a few minutes, or a few years, and you will know more about Zen than a million books can teach.

Dogen: To sit properly, first lay down a thick pillow and on top of this a second (round) one. One may sit either in the full or half cross-legged position. In the full position, one places the right foot on the left thigh and the left foot on the right thigh. In the half position, only the left foot is placed upon the right thigh. Robe and belt should be worn loosely, but in order. The right hand rests on the left foot, while the back of the left hand rests on the palm of the right. The two thumbs are placed in juxtaposition. Let the body be kept upright, leaning neither to the left nor to the right, neither forward nor backward.

Ears and shoulders, nose and navel must be aligned to one another. The tongue is to be kept against the palate, lips, and teeth firmly closed, while the eyes should always be left open.

Now that the bodily position is in order, regulate your breathing. If a wish arises, take note of it and then dismiss it. If you practice in this way for a long time, you will forget all attachments and concentration will come naturally. That is the art of Zazen. Zazen is the **dharma** gate of great rest and joy.

Alice: What does one think about while doing Zazen?

Dogen: One thinks about nothing.

Alice: How does one think of not thinking?

Dogen: Without thinking.

Alice: But Buddhism was a foreign import on Japanese soil. Did the Japanese, like the Chinese, eventually tire of it?

Caterpillar: No. But they tried to discover the original Japanese feeling of spirituality, before Chinese influences.

MOTOORI NORINAGA

Though Japan created its own spins on Buddhist, Confucian, and Taoist thought, more interesting than these Chinese transplants are those Japanese philosophers who attempted to free Japanese spirituality from these Chinese influences.

One such thinker was **Motoori Norinaga** (1730-1801). He felt that the Japanese should return to the *Way of the Kami.* And he wrote and lectured on the original Japanese spiritual qualities present in Japanese literature, especially in:

1 *The Man'yoshu, Collection of Myriad Leaves, (750 A.D.):*
The most ancient collection of poetry. The Man'yoshu provides one of the few literary sources for knowledge prior to the Chinese-ization of Japanese culture in the T'ang dynasty. The Man'yoshu was important to Norinaga because it contained "original" Japanese feelings and sentiments:

> **The waves rock the kelp beds**
> **Like wings quivering in the evening.**
> **Just as the sea tangle sways**
> **and floats**
> **At one with the waves,**
> **So my girl clung to me**
> **As she lay by my side.**

2 _The Tale of Genji:_ A novel written by Lady Murasaki. It concerns the amorous life of Prince Genji and his many loves, including Murasaki herself. It is still regarded by many as Japan's greatest novel:

> **The troubled waters are**
> **frozen fast.**
> **Under clear heaven**
> **moonlight and shadow**
> **ebb and flow.**

> **The memories of long love**
> **gather like drifting snow,**
> **poignant as the mandarin**
> **ducks**
> **who float side by side in sleep.**

3 _The Kojiki (The Records of Ancient Matters):_ The most ancient records of Japanese myth and history. It tells of the primal pair Izanagi and Izanami giving birth to Japan's eight islands, of the birth of the Sun Goddess Amaterasu from the left eye of Izanagi, and of the descent of the line of emperors from these primordial, mythic ancestors.

The two Deities, standing upon the Floating Bridge of Heaven, pushed down the jewelled spear and stirred with it, whereupon, when they had stirred the brine till it went curdle-curdle and drew the spear up, the brine that dripped down from the end of the spear was piled up and became an island—the Island of Onogoro.

For Norinaga, there is no concept more important than that of **mono no aware**. In fact, mono no aware is probably the most important aesthetic concept in all of Japanese culture. **Aware** is a feeling of awe, a feeling for the "**awe**ness of things." In the early poetry of the Man'yoshu, aware describes the melancholy songs of birds and crickets. Later, it meant a gentle sorrow, a sensitivity to beauty and its impermanence.

The flowers whirl away
In the wind like snow.
The thing that falls away
Is myself.

If one is without real, deep human emotion, then one will not have a sense of this "pathos of things." According to Norinaga, deep human feeling is feminine and weak.

Doesn't he realize that I am not
like the swaying kelp where the
*   seaweed gatherer*
can come as often as he wants.

But wise men are in touch with this deep and weak feminine, emotive nature. Norinaga, then, was not concerned with the Buddhist notion that poetry can help one gain enlightenment. He was not concerned with enlightenment at all, but only with deep feeling:

> **The cricket cries**
> **In the frost.**
> **On my narrow bed,**
> **In a folded quilt,**
> **I sleep alone.**

Things which move us deeply can be either good or evil—and we have no control over what grips us deeply. Norinaga also felt that the Japanese should return to what he calls **Natural Shinto—the Shinto of the Age of the Gods**—not the contemporary form of Shinto which had been corrupted by Confucian and Buddhist ideas.

Alice: What were some more of the Buddhist schools?

PURE LAND BUDDHISM

Caterpillar: In Japan, **Pure Land Buddhism** is known as *Judo*. Just as the Chinese took delight in chanting *O-mi-t'o-fo*, the Japanese Judo sect not only chanted the name of Amitaba, but danced in the streets to the chant, with the accompaniment of drums. One famous Judo master even danced and chanted, naked in the streets.

In fact, the poet **Issa** satirized those Pure Land Buddhists who placed all their faith in the chant, but were immoral, even murderous, Buddhists:

> Every time a Pure Land Buddhist
> Swats a fly,
> **"Namu Amida Butsu!"**
> Is his cry.

Nichiren Buddhism

Caterpillar: Though Pure Land Buddhism has the largest number of followers in Japan today, **Nichiren** is second.

Nichiren (1222-1282) was a Japanese Buddhist monk who taught that the only way to attain enlightenment in the current age is to recite the title of the **Lotus Sutra**: "**Namu myoho renge kyo**", or "I take refuge in the Lotus of the Wonderful Law Sutra."

In his essay, "Treatise on the Establishment of Righteousness to Secure the Peace of the State," he criticized the government for not accepting his form of Buddhism as the only true religion. He predicted (accurately) that Japan would be invaded unless the entire country was converted. Like much of Japanese religion, Nichiren Buddhism is nationalistic-and this-worldly, and fond of chanting.

Nichiren: Mundane existence is nothing but Nirvana. Man and woman, in copulation, chant "namu myo ho renge kyo." Thus, affliction is nothing but enlightenment, mundane existence, nothing but Nirvana.

Caterpillar: In this way, the Japanese simplified Chinese Buddhism. Instead of engaging in long philosophical debates, as the Indian and Chinese Buddhists did, each Buddhist school delivered a simple message:

> PURE LAND (Judo Shu): **Chant namu Amida Butsu**
> NICHIREN: **Chant namu myo ho renge kyo.**
> ZEN: **Don't chant. Don't think. Meditate.**

THE PHILOSOPHIES AND RELIGIONS OF TIBET

TIBETAN BUDDHISM

ntering Big Sur is like entering a Chinese landscape painting. Pearly dragons of fog curl around dark mountainous headlands plunging headlong into laboring seas studded with jade coves and strewn with trunks of fallen redwoods. In the 1960s, along the stream banks up the canyons, hippies hovered around campfires, surrounded by the sweet scent of marijuana, guitar riffs from Marakesh and Goa, and the muffled thunder of a distant waterfall. Rachaels and Jennifers with trailing braids, having bathed their limbs in pools fed by waterfalls, stood between the gloomy redwoods, robed only in golden, slanting shafts of light, combing out their hair. At night, moonlight played upon their faces as they scratched love poems on the backs of their lovers, their shaken anklets tinkling with little silver bells.

The real Mecca, however, was not Big Sur. After all, the only space in the universe that really mattered, was the Void. The Void was not a geographical space, but a psychological, spiritual one—and many hippie conversations eventually got around to the question: "Have you seen the Void? The Great White Light?" It was supposed to be the hippest space ever.

And if you were spiritually "high," you pretended that you had been there. Thus, upon awakening, those same Jennifers and Rachaels and their Christ-eyed lovers would fast, ingest an elephant's dose of LSD, and, as their private worlds began melting into molten flows of paisley lights, they closed their eyes and contemplated the lyrics of a Beatles tune, taken from the *Tibetan Book of the Dead*:

> **Turn off your mind,**
> **Relax, and float downstream.**
> **It is not dying,**
> **It is not dying.**
> **Lay down all thought,**
> **Surrender to the Void.**
> **It is shining.**
> **It is shining.**
> **That you may see**
> **The meaning of within.**
> **It is being.**
> **It is being...**

When a Tibetan monk dies, he is read to from the same book—the **Bardo To-drol**—in Tibetan. His spirit, residing in the Intermediate State, or Bardo, between incarnations, is at that time assaulted by a stream of hallucinogenic visions: wrathful deities and peaceful deities in swirling arrays of light and sound.

If the monk can enter the Great White Light from which the flow of images emanates, he gains enlightenment, and does not get reborn. But if he fails to do so, then the desire for a new body arises, and he follows smoky lights into the Bardo of Seeking Rebirth. In this Bardo he views his past life, and the Lord of Death weighs his good deeds with white pebbles and his bad deeds with black ones.

Then, the actions of his previous existences propel him towards an appropriate womb, so that he will be reborn in an environment suitable to his karma. As he approaches the womb he sees visions of men and women making love. If the soul is jealous towards the male and is attracted to the mother, he will gain a male body. If attracted to the father, and jealous of the mother, the soul will attain a female body. Then different landscapes will appear, and the soul will be propelled towards one, perhaps in Big Sur...

Meanwhile, back in Tibet, whorls of incense curl through a monastery like flying dragons. Seated Buddha-like in long maroon robes and flamboyant hats, monks chant in a deep, resonant bullfrog-like monotone, their hands gesturing like those of a hula dancer in freeze-frame. To spice things up, they occasionally pound on a drum made of a human skull, or blow on a trumpet fashioned of a human thigh bone.

These are Tibetan Buddhists, followers of a Tantric branch of Buddhism known as **Vajrayana**. According to Tibetans, Vajrayana is the speedy path to enlightenment, allowing one to attain Nirvana in a single lifetime. To this end, they employ:

- ≋ **Mantras**: sacred sounds that are the resonant body of living Gods and Goddesses.
- ≋ **Mudras:** Sacred hand gestures.
- ≋ **Mandalas**: Sacred icons.

The monks, as their chanting deepens, visualize the Goddess whose mantra they are chanting, then merge with her in their minds.

Presiding over all of this is the **Dalai Lama**. Tibetans believe him to be an incarnation of the **Bodhisattva**, who in India is known as **Avalokitsehvara**, and in China is known as **Kuan Yin**. In Tibet he is called **Chenrezig**. There he is both the political and spiritual leader of the Tibetans, who offer him absolute submission.

The present Dalai Lama, **Tenzin Byatso**, is the fourteenth. Born in 1935, the year radar was invented and the song "Blue Moon" was popular on the American airwaves, he was only 15 when the Chinese invaded his homeland in 1950. In 1959 he fled his country, and set up his government-in-exile in Dharamsala, India. Meanwhile, the Chinese government has killed over a million Tibetans, imprisoned thousands of monks and nuns, destroyed monasteries, pursued an oppressive policy against women, which included forced abortions and intermarriage, used Tibet for nuclear testing and disposal of nuclear wastes, and chopped down 50 percent of Tibet's forests.

The Dalai Lama's nonviolent resistance to these atrocities earned him the Nobel Peace Prize in 1989. Since then, he has won popular attention in two movies, *Seven Years in Tibet* and *Kundun*. Nevertheless, no government has been willing to risk losing their trade status with China over Tibetan rights. The Chinese market seems to be more valuable to the world than Tibetan freedom.

BON

Buddhism was not Tibet's first religion, however. It was **Bon**, based on a belief that the world is filled with countless spirits. These spirits can cause good fortune or ill fortune. Of course, there are shamans who can communicate with these spirits. The spirits take over the body and mind of a medium and utter commands and prophecies. Today, the Bon and Tibetan Buddhist religions are thoroughly intermixed.

Alice: I feel a little confused. There are so many philosophies in the East, I hardly know which one to follow!

Krishnamurti: There are laws in some countries, I believe, which prohibit anyone from following you in the street and if someone does he can be arrested and put into prison. So, spiritually, I wish there were a police system which would put people into a spiritual prison for following others. In fact, it does happen automatically.

Alice: But if I take that seriously, then aren't I following you?

Krishnamurti: The state of mind that questions is much more important than the question itself. Any question may be asked by a slavish mind, and the answer it receives will still be within the limitation of its own slavery...Freedom of desire for an answer is essential for the understanding of a problem.

Index.

Bibliography

Cheng, Hsueh-li. *Empty Logic: Madhyamika Buddhism from Chinese Sources.* Motilal Banarsidas, 1991.

Coward. Harold. *Derrida and Indian Philosophy.* SUNY Press, 1990.

Cross, Steven. *The Elements of Hinduism.* Element, 1994.

Dalai Lama. *The World of Tibetan Buddhism: An Overview of Its Philosophy and Practice.* Wisdom, 1995

DeBary, William Theodore. *The Buddhist Tradition.* Modern Library, 1964.
— ed. *Sources of Indian Tradition.* Columbia University Press, 1958
— ed. *Sources of Japanese Tradition.* Columbia University Press, 1964.

Flood, Gavin. *An Introduction to Hinduism.* Cambridge University Press, 1996.

Hopkins, Jeffrey. *Emptiness Yoga.* Snow Lion, 1987.

Huntington, C. W., Jr. *The Emptiness of Emptiness.* University of Hawaii Press, 1989.

Katsuki, Sekida. *Zen Training: Methods and Philosophy.* Weatherhill, 1975.

Klostermaier, Klaus K. *A Survey of Hinduism.* SUNY Press, 1994.

Larson, Gerald James (M.-L.). *India's Agony Over Religion.* SUNY Press, 1995.

Mallory, J. P. *In Search of the Indo-Europeans: Language, Archaeology, Myth.* Thames and Hudson, 1989.

Radhakrishnan, S. and Moore, C. eds. *A Sourcebook in Indian Philosophy.* Princeton University Press, 1967.

Said, Edward. *Orientalism.* Vintage, 1979.

Stoddart, William. *Outline of Hinduism.* The Foundation for Traditional Studies, 1993.

Suzuki, D.T. *Zen and Japanese Culture.* Princeton University Press, 1959.

Thomas, Barry. *Buddhism.* Hawthorne, 1965.

Yu, Lu Kuan. *Taoist Yoga: Alchemy and Immortality.* Weiser, 1973.

Zaehner, R. C., *Hindu Scriptures.* Dutton, 1966.

Jim Powell

Jim Powell lives in Santa Barbara, California where he enjoys surfing, writing, playing piano and painting.

His other books include Mandalas: *The Dynamics of Vedic Symbolism*; *Energy and Eros*; *The Tao of Symbols*; *Derrida for Beginners* and *Postmodernism for Beginners*. Jim has a Master's Degree in Religious Studies with an emphasis on Sanskrit and Indology. His thesis was on Vedic mythology. He also holds a Master's Degree in English Literature, and wrote a thesis on Mark Twain's relationshipship with the Mississippi River. His web page is:

www.west.net/~coyote/books.html

Joe Lee

Joe Lee is an illustrator, cartoonist, writer and clown. A graduate of Ringling Brothers, Barnum and Bailey's Clown College, he worked for many years as a circus clown. He is the author and illustrator of Writers and Readers' *The History of Clowns for Beginners* and *Dante for Beginners*, and the illustrator of *Jung*, *Postmodernism* and *Shakespeare* titles in this same series. Joe lives in Bloomington, Indiana with his wife, Mary Bess, three cats and Toby, the fox terror.